New Or

day B

_____ glasses

_____ discs/disks

__1__ maps

__1__ bks/pamphs

3rd Edition

WITHDRAWN

by Julia Kamysz Lane

FrommerMedia LLC

Contents

Published by:

FrommerMedia LLC

ISBN: 978-1-62887-025-1 (paper); 978-1-62887-055-8 (ebk)

Editorial Director: Pauline Frommer
Editor: Kate Hambrecht
Production Editor: Jana M. Stefanciosa
Photo Editor: Meghan Lamb
Cartographer: Tim Lohnes
Page Compositor: Lissa Auciello-Brogan
Indexer: Cheryl Lenser

For information on our other products and services, please contact Support@FrommerMedia.com..

About This Book

Organizing your time. That's what this guide is all about.

Other guides give you long lists of things to see and do and then expect you to fit the pieces together. The Day by Day guides are different. These guides tell you the best of everything, and then they show you how to see it *in the smartest, most time-efficient way.*

Our authors have designed detailed itineraries organized by time, neighborhood, or special interest. And each tour comes with a bulleted map that takes you from stop to stop.

Hoping to soak in the history of the French Quarter, visit some underwater friends at the Aquarium of the Americas, or see where some of the U.S.'s most famous writers spent their time and spun their tales? Planning a walk through the Garden District, or dinner and drinks where you can dance the night away to a local jazz or brass band? Whatever your interest or schedule, the Day by Days give you the smartest routes to follow. Not only do we take you to the top attractions, hotels, and restaurants, but we also help you access those special moments that locals get to experience—those "finds" that turn tourists into travelers.

The Day by Days are also your top choice if you're looking for one complete guide for all your travel needs. The best hotels and restaurants for every budget, the greatest shopping values, the wildest nightlife—it's all here.

Why should you trust our judgment? Because our authors personally visit each place they write about. They're an independent lot who say what they think and would never include places they wouldn't recommend to their best friends. They're also open to suggestions from readers. If you'd like to contact them, please send your comments our way at Support@FrommerMedia.com, and we'll pass them on.

Enjoy your Day by Day guide—the most helpful travel companion you can buy. And have the trip of a lifetime.

About the Author

Julia Kamysz Lane divides her time between a 1940s cottage in New Orleans and an old farmhouse in northern Illinois. She and her husband enjoy Southern cooking, historic architecture, and books. They share their home with four dogs and two cats, and are expecting their first child.

An Additional Note

Please be advised that travel information is subject to change at any time—and this is especially true of prices. We therefore suggest that you write or call ahead for confirmation when making your travel plans. The authors, editors, and publisher cannot be held responsible for the experiences of readers while traveling. Your safety is important to us, however, so we encourage you to stay alert and be aware of your surroundings.

Star Ratings, Icons & Abbreviations

Every hotel, restaurant, and attraction listing in this guide has been ranked for quality, value, service, amenities, and special features using a **star-rating system.** Hotels, restaurants, attractions, shopping, and nightlife are rated on a scale of zero stars (recommended) to three stars (exceptional). In addition to the star-rating system, we also use a **kids** **icon** to point out the best bets for families. Within each tour, we recommend cafes, bars, or restaurants where you can take a break. Each of these stops appears in a shaded box marked with a coffee-cup-shaped bullet ☕.

The following **abbreviations** are used for credit cards:

AE	American Express	DISC	Discover	V	Visa
DC	Diners Club	MC	MasterCard		

Frommers.com

Frommer's travel resources don't end with this guide. Frommer's website, **www.frommers.com,** has travel information on more than 4,000 destinations. We update features regularly, giving you access to the most current trip-planning information and the best airfare, lodging, and car-rental bargains. You can also listen to podcasts, connect with other Frommers.com members through our active-reader forums, share your travel photos, read blogs from guidebook editors and fellow travelers, and much more.

A Note on Prices

In the "Take a Break" and "Best Bets" sections of this book, we have used a system of dollar signs to show a range of costs for 1 night in a hotel (the price of a double-occupancy room) or the cost of an entree at a restaurant. Use the following table to decipher the dollar signs:

Cost	Hotels	Restaurants
$	under $130	under $15
$$	$130–$200	$15–$30
$$$	$200–$300	$30–$40
$$$$	$300–$395	$40–$50
$$$$$	over $395	over $50

How to Contact Us

In researching this book, we discovered many wonderful places—hotels, restaurants, shops, and more. We're sure you'll find others. Please tell us about them, so we can share the information with your fellow travelers in upcoming editions. If you were disappointed with a recommendation, we'd love to know that, too. Please write to: Support@FrommerMedia.com

16 Favorite
Moments

16 Favorite **Moments**

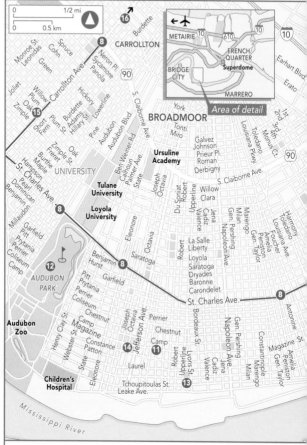

1. Café du Monde
2. Jackson Square
3. Le Petit Théâtre
4. Ferry to Algiers Point
5. Snug Harbor
6. Napoleon House
7. Louisiana Music Factory
8. National World War II Museum
9. St. Charles streetcar
10. Mardi Gras Parade
    (not mapped; see p. 34)
11. Guy's
12. Audubon Park
13. Hansen's Sno-Bliz
14. Magazine Street shops
15. Rue de la Course
16. Mid City Rock 'n' Bowl

Previous page: Jackson Square with the Cabildo, St. Louis Cathedral, and the Presbytere (from left to right) in the background.

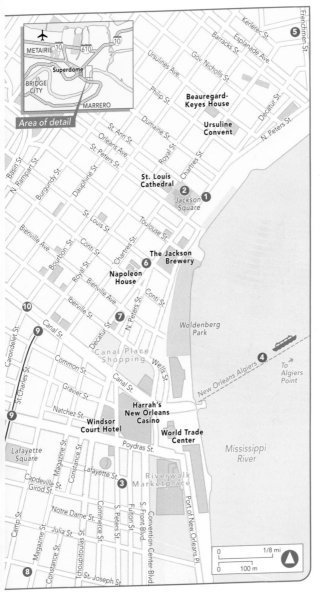

METAIRIE

Superdome

BRIDGE
CITY

MARRERO

Area of detail

Kerlerec St.

Frenchmen St.

Barracks St.

Esplanade Ave.

Gov. Nicholls St.

Ursulines Ave.

Philip St.

Beauregard-
Keyes House

Dumaine St.

Ursuline
Convent

Decatur St.

N. Peters St.

St. Ann St.

Orleans Ave.

St. Peters St.

Royal St.

Chartres St.

Basin St.

N. Rampart St.

Burgundy St.

Dauphine St.

St. Louis
Cathedral

Jackson
Square

St. Louis St.

Toulouse St.

Bienville Ave.

Conti St.

Chartres St.

The Jackson
Brewery

Bourbon St.

Royal St.

Napoleon
House

Bienville Ave.

Conti St.

Ibenville St.

N. Peters St.

Canal St.

Woldenberg
Park

Carondelet St.

St. Charles St.

Canal Place
Shopping

Wells St.

New Orleans Algiers

To
Algiers
Point

Common St.

Canal St.

Gravier St.

Natchez St.

Harrah's
New Orleans
Casino

Windsor
Court Hotel

World Trade
Center

Mississippi
River

Lafayette
Square

Poydras St.

Magazine St.

Constance St.

Lafayette St.

Riverwalk
Marketplace

Capdeville St.

Girod St.

Notre Dame St.

Commerce St.

S. Peters St.

Fulton St.

Convention Center Blvd.

Port of New Orleans Pl.

Camp St.

Magazine St.

Julia St.

Tchoupitoulas St.

Constance St.

St. Joseph St.

0   1/8 mi

0   100 m

New Orleans is called the **City that Care Forgot.** And it is indeed easy to let go of your troubles while swaying with the crowd at a parade or feasting on fresh seafood in a little family restaurant. All of your senses are delighted in the Crescent City, whether hearing the soulful notes of a saxophone or feeling gentle drops of rain cool you off on a warm afternoon. Locals are famous for welcoming visitors as one of their own and inviting them to indulge in everything New Orleans has to offer. So don't be afraid to let loose and *laissez les bon temps rouler!* For ideas on how to start doing just that, check out some of my favorite New Orleans moments below.

Passengers aboard the ferry to Algiers Point enjoy views of the New Orleans skyline.

1 **Bite into a beignet at world-famous Café du Monde.** You'll never be so happy to get coated in powdered sugar! Don't forget the creamy café au lait. See p 48.

2 **People-watch in Jackson Square.** Stroll the heart of the French Quarter, which pulses night and day with talented street musicians, eclectic artists, funny mimes, and passionate fortune-tellers. Most of the entertainment is free, but if you like what you see or hear, drop a few coins in the hat. See p 9.

3 **Enjoy a performance at Le Petit Théâtre,** housed in an intimate 1920s Spanish-style dwelling with cushy red seats to sink into. The nearly 100-year-old community theater is renowned for classics by Southern playwrights such as Tennessee Williams. See p 132.

4 **Ferry across the Mississippi River to Algiers Point,** one of New Orleans's oldest suburbs and home to jazz pioneers, for a dramatic perspective on the city skyline. See p 92.

5 **Snap your fingers to live jazz at Snug Harbor,** the place to hear legends like pianist Ellis Marsalis, father of Pulitzer Prize–winning composer/trumpeter Wynton Marsalis, and power vocalist Charmaine Neville. See p 120.

A bust of Napoleon sits above the cash register at Napoleon House.

A ride on the St. Charles streetcar is a fun and cheap way to get a passing view of the Garden District.

6 Say cheers with a Pimm's Cup at Napoleon House, a bar and café in a 200-year-old mansion once offered by New Orleans mayor Nicholas Girod as refuge for the exiled French emperor. Napoleon never took up Mayor Girod on his hospitality, but a bust of the Little Corporal serves as fine company for the patrons, many of them artists and writers who aspire to take over the world in their own way. *See p 120.*

7 Flip through vintage vinyl while tapping toes to weekly live concerts at Louisiana Music Factory, a beloved 21-year-old independent record store in the French Quarter. Choose from thousands of new and used LPs, CDs, tapes, and DVDs, with an emphasis on jazz, blues, R & B, Cajun and zydeco. *See p 82.*

8 Climb into a Higgins landing craft at the National World War II Museum. The boat that made victory possible on D-Day was invented and built in New Orleans and tested on the brackish waters of Lake Pontchartrain. *See p 81.*

9 Ride the St. Charles streetcar. Marvel at the world-famous St. Charles Avenue's historic mansions, universities, churches, and temples. There's no better way to cool off on a warm day than the breeze through a streetcar window as you travel beneath a sweeping canopy of live oaks. *See p 17.*

10 Yell, "Throw me something, mister!" at a Mardi Gras parade. Then test your hand-eye coordination while catching beads, doubloons, and other throws. Remember that beads beget beads, so throw a few pearls around your neck before you hear the police sirens announcing the start of the parade. *See p 34.*

A member of the Zulus prepares to make his "throws."

No one can resist a snoball from Hansen's Sno-Bliz.

sprawling live oaks dripping with Spanish moss make for a particularly romantic scene. *See p 86.*

⓭ **Cool off with a snoball at Hansen's Sno-Bliz.** No slushies or slurpies here! The late Mary's original syrups make for endlessly sticky sweet (or sour) combinations. *See p 86.*

⓮ **Explore the shops of Magazine Street,** 6 glorious miles (9.6km) of antiques, books, vintage clothing, and more. I have yet to meet any shopaholic who can go the distance in one day, but you'll have fun trying. *See p 18.*

⓫ **Savor the signature grilled shrimp po' boy at Guy's,** a small family-run eatery favored by locals. Grab a bottle of Barq's from the corner cooler and glance through *Gambit*, the local alternative newspaper, while you wait for your freshly made order. *See p 105.*

⓬ **Stroll through Audubon Park** and look for wood ducks, egrets, cranes, and sunbathing turtles that plop back into the water if you get too close. The still lagoons and

⓯ **Sip an iced cioccolato at Rue de la Course,** one of my favorite independent coffeehouses ever. It's in a cavernous former bank at Carrollton and Oak that features a second-story loft from which you can better view the 19th-century architectural details and unusually eclectic patrons. *See p 72.*

⓰ **Bowl to live zydeco music at Mid City Rock 'n' Bowl.** It's not much to look at from the outside, but go up the steps to discover a unique venue where you can dance, drink, and bowl all at the same time. *See p 15.* ●

Rue de la Course is a delightful coffee shop housed in a former bank building.

The Best in One Day

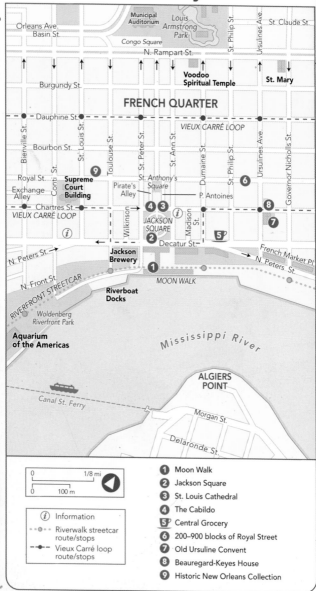

Orleans Ave.
Basin St.
Municipal Auditorium
Louis Armstrong Park
Congo Square
N. Rampart St.
St. Philip St.
Ursulines Ave.
St. Claude St.

Burgundy St.
Voodoo Spiritual Temple
St. Mary

FRENCH QUARTER

Dauphine St.
VIEUX CARRÉ LOOP

Bienville St.
St. Louis St.
Bourbon St.
Toulouse St.
St. Peter St.
St. Ann St.
Dumaine St.
St. Philip St.
Ursulines Ave.
Governor Nicholls St.

Royal St.
Exchange Alley
Conti St.
Supreme Court Building
Pirate's Alley
St. Anthony's Square
P. Antoines
❾
❻
Chartres St.
VIEUX CARRÉ LOOP
❹ ❸
JACKSON SQUARE
Madison St.
ⓘ
❽
❼
❷
Decatur St.
Wilkinson
❺
Jackson Brewery
French Market Pl.
N. Peters St.
❶
N. Peters St.
MOON WALK
N. Front St.
RIVERFRONT STREETCAR
Riverboat Docks
Woldenberg Riverfront Park
Aquarium of the Americas

Mississippi River

ALGIERS POINT

Canal St. Ferry
Morgan St.
Delaronde St.

0 — 1/8 mi
0 — 100 m

ⓘ Information
••○•• Riverwalk streetcar route/stops
–•–•– Vieux Carré loop route/stops

❶ Moon Walk
❷ Jackson Square
❸ St. Louis Cathedral
❹ The Cabildo
❺ Central Grocery
❻ 200–900 blocks of Royal Street
❼ Old Ursuline Convent
❽ Beauregard-Keyes House
❾ Historic New Orleans Collection

Previous page: A trumpet player blows his horn in front of St. Louis Cathedral.

If you only have 1 day in New Orleans, go to the heart of the city, the world-famous French Quarter. As you walk under wrought-iron balconies and steal glances through brick arches to private courtyards, you'll let go of everyday concerns and embrace a simpler time. Here, you can find anything you desire, from elegant antiques to alligator heads. START: **Moon Walk, across from Jackson Square.**

1 kids Moon Walk. The sleepy riverside park, which winds along the Mississippi River, is a tribute to former mayor Maurice Edwin "Moon" Landrieu, during whose administration it was built. 🕐 *20 min. Across from Jackson Square along Mississippi River. Go before 8pm for safety's sake.*

2 ★ kids Jackson Square. In the days when it was known as the Plaza de Armas, military parades and public executions were common. On November 30, 1803, citizens gathered here to learn that Louisiana was once again a French possession. But less than a month later, the people were told of the Louisiana Purchase, marking America's cheapest and largest land grab of all time. These days, you'll find

A sign in Jackson Square noting the former Spanish name of the square, Plaza de Armas.

artists displaying paintings and drawings, palm readers telling fortunes, and little kids tap-dancing for spare change. 🕐 *30 min.–1 hr. Fronts the 700 block of Decatur St. and is bounded by Chartres, St. Ann,*

St. Louis Cathedral.

A display case exhibiting relics of old New Orleans in the Cabildo.

and St. Peter sts. www.explorenew
orleans.com. Dawn–dusk.

③ ★★ St. Louis Cathedral. New
Orleans is home to one of the
South's largest Catholic popula-
tions and boasts the oldest continu-
ously operating cathedral in the
U.S. This is the third building to
have stood on this spot; a 1722 hurricane demolished the first, and the
great fire of 1788 burned the second. Supposedly the church's bells
were not rung as a warning of the

fire because it was Good Friday.
🕐 *20 min. 615 Pere Antoine Alley.*
☎ *504/525-9585. www.stlouis
cathedral.org. Mon–Sat 9am–4pm,
Sun 9am–2pm. Mass schedule online.*

④ ★ The Cabildo. Originally built
in 1795 as the Spanish seat of government, this is the site where the
French turned over the Louisiana
Purchase to the U.S. in 1803. Despite
the ravages of time and a fire in the
1980s, the Cabildo lives on, educating visitors on what it took to

Inside the Beauregard-Keyes House.

survive in 18th-century Louisiana. ① *1 hr. 701 Chartres St.* ☎ *800/568-6968 or 504/568-6968. www.crt.state.la.us/museum/properties/cabildo. Admission $6 adults, $5 students and seniors, free children 12 and under. Tues–Sun 10am–4:30pm.*

5 Central Grocery. Stop by this grocery for one of its famously filling muffuletta sandwiches. You can also buy many New Orleans spices and other deli items here. *923 Decatur St.* ☎ *504/523-1620. $.*

6 200–900 blocks of Royal Street. If rowdy Bourbon Street is the black sheep of the French Quarter, then Royal Street is its prim and proper cousin, boasting fine-art galleries, antiques shops, women's clothing boutiques, and home-accessory nooks. For a detailed map of shops along Royal Street, turn to p 75. ① *90 min.*

7 ★★ Old Ursuline Convent. The convent was built in 1752 by the Sisters of Ursula, who came to New Orleans from France and opened the first girls' school in the U.S. in 1727. From 1831 to 1834, the Louisiana state legislature was based here. Today the building houses a Catholic archive with documents dating back to 1718. ① *1–1½ hr. 1100 Chartres St.* ☎ *504/529-3040. www.oldursulineconvent.org. Admission $5 adults, $4 seniors, $3 students, free children 6 and under. Mon–Sat 10am–4pm.*

8 ★ Beauregard-Keyes House. Built in 1826, this stunning raised Greek Revival home is named for its most famous tenants: Confederate General Pierre Gustave Toutant Beauregard, who resided here after the Civil War, and author Frances Parkinson Keyes (pronounced *cause*), who wrote many of her novels here, including the most well-known, *Dinner at Antoine's.* The landscaped courtyard opens to the former servants' quarters, where Keyes maintained her writing space. The beautifully restored formal garden is a breathtaking oasis. Note the twin staircases, Doric columns, and the "raised cottage" architecture. ① *1 hr. 1113 Chartres St.* ☎ *504/523-7257. www.bkhouse.org. Admission $10 adults, $9 students and seniors, $4 children 6–12, free children 5 and under. Mon–Sat 10am–3pm.*

9 ★ Historic New Orleans Collection. A complex of late-18th- and early-19th-century buildings tells the story of New Orleans's past and present through changing exhibits on art, food, architecture, music, and more. ① *45 min. 533 Royal St.* ☎ *504/523-4662. www.hnoc.org. Free admission for self-guided tours, $5 docent tours. Tues–Sat 9:30am–4:30pm; Sun 10:30am–4:30pm.*

Historic New Orleans Collection.

The Best in Two Days

1. City Park
2. New Orleans Museum of Art
3. New Orleans Botanical Garden
4. Bayou St. John
5. Pitot House
6. Canal streetcar
7. Sacred Grinds
8. Hurricane Katrina Memorial
9. Cypress Grove & Greenwood cemeteries
10. Lake Lawn Cemetery
11. Mid City Rock 'n' Bowl

Area of detail

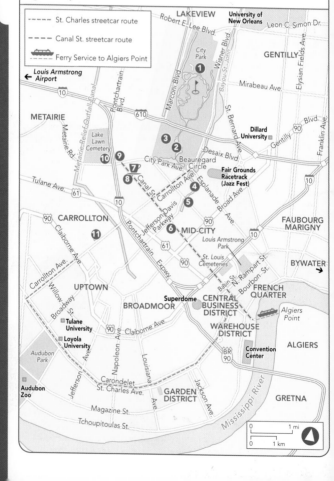

---- St. Charles streetcar route

---- Canal St. streetcar route

🚢 Ferry Service to Algiers Point

From the feel-good food to the thought-provoking art and architecture, Mid-City is where it's at, y'all. The Mid-City neighborhood was devastated by Hurricane Katrina flooding in 2005, but walking among homes, schools, and businesses in various stages of renewal, you'll get a feel for what New Orleans is all about—community spirit, tenacity, and pride. START: **Canal streetcar, City Park/Museum car.**

1 ★★ **City Park.** Play golf or tennis, or go horseback riding, fishing, birding, or boating. Kids will clamor to go on the antique wooden carousel at the Carousel Gardens Amusement Park or climb through, over, and under the fairy-tale sculptures at Storyland. See p 88. ⏱ *1 hr. 1 Palm Dr.; bounded by City Park Ave. and Canal, Lee, and Wisner boulevards.* ☎ *504/482-4888. www.neworleanscitypark.com. Open daily.*

2 **New Orleans Museum of Art.** City Park's main oak-lined entrance also leads directly to NOMA, home to priceless paintings and sculptures and one of the largest fine photography collections in the region. ⏱ *2–3 hr. 1 Collins Diboll Circle.* ☎ *504/658-4100. www.noma.org. Admission $10 adults, $8 seniors and students with I.D., $6 children 7–17, free children 6 and under and local students. Tues–Thurs 10am–6pm; Fri 10am–9pm; Sat–Sun 11am–5pm.*

City Park.

New Orleans Botanical Garden.

3 kids **New Orleans Botanical Garden.** Originally created as part of the Works Progress Administration in the 1930s, this public garden still has many of its original Art Deco flourishes. Explore 12 acres (4.8 hectares) of gardens, fountains, ponds, and sculptures, plus a horticultural library and a gift shop. Kids of all ages will especially enjoy the miniature train garden (only on weekends). ⏱ *1 hr. 3 Victory Ave., behind the New Orleans Museum of Art.* ☎ *504/483-9386. www.neworleanscitypark.com/botanical-garden. Admission $6 adults, $3 children 5–12, free for children 4 and under. Tues–Sun 10am–4:30pm.*

As you leave City Park, cross Wisner Boulevard and go over the bridge. Turn right on Moss Street and you'll be on the west side of Bayou St. John.

4 ★ **Bayou St. John.** This historic waterway once connected Lake Pontchartrain to the Mississippi River, serving as an important

Bayou St. John.

channel for Native Americans and, later, European explorers. However, modern development swallowed up parts of the bayou, so it no longer connects the two. What remains serves as a popular recreational spot for fishing, canoeing, and bird-watching. See p 66. ○ *30 min.*

⑤ ★ Pitot House. Enter the romantic grounds of this 18th-century Creole colonial house museum and you can easily imagine the lives of New Orleans's earliest settlers. The city's first American mayor, James Pitot, lived here from 1810 to 1819. Back then, it was considered to be a country home, which gives you an idea of how much development the bayou spawned

over the past two centuries. ○ *1 hr. 1440 Moss St.* ☎ *504/482-0312. www.pitothouse.org. Admission $7 adults, $5 students, seniors, and children 7–18, free children 6 and under. Wed–Sat 10am–3pm.*

⑥ ★ 🅺🅸🅳🆂 Canal Streetcar. Unlike those of the historic St. Charles line, the Canal cars are bright red and feature air-conditioning and wheelchair access. They might lack character, but that cool air will feel good on a hot, humid afternoon. Be sure to grab the car that says "Cemeteries." ○ *30 min. Jefferson Davis Parkway at Canal St.* ☎ *504/ 827-7970. www.norta.com. $1.25 one-way fare.*

⑦ Sacred Grinds. At the end of the streetcar line, you'll find Sacred Grinds Coffee House, with relaxed outdoor seating where you can cool off with an iced coffee or one of its frozen Chill'ems (the Dirty Zombie is my fave). Enjoy a generous helping of quiche or pastry to fuel your venture into the neighboring "Cities of the Dead." *5055 Canal St.* ☎ *504/488-4889. $.*

Family tombs at Cypress Grove Cemetery.

A band plays at Mid City Lanes Rock 'n' Bowl, a beloved New Orleans institution.

8 ★ **Hurricane Katrina Memorial.** Charity Hospital's long-neglected pauper's field has been transformed into a tranquil resting place for the 85 unclaimed victims of Hurricane Katrina's levee breaks. The memorial includes the names of all who lost their lives in the 2005 tragedy. ⓘ *20 min. 5056 Canal St.* ☎ *504/568-3201.*

9 ★ **Cypress Grove & Greenwood cemeteries.** Firemen's Charitable & Benevolent Association founded Cypress Grove Cemetery in 1840 to honor its courageous volunteer firemen. At the entrance, you'll find the massive 1840 vaults of Perseverance Fire Co. No. 13. The yellow fever epidemic of 1852 hit New Orleans particularly hard; Greenwood Cemetery was opened that same year to alleviate overcrowding at Cypress Grove. Both cemeteries contain some of the finest memorial architecture in the world, featuring marble, granite, and cast-iron tombs. ⓘ *90 min. 5200 Canal Blvd.* ☎ *504/482-8983. www.greenwoodnola.com. Free admission. Daily 8am–4pm.*

10 ★★ **Lake Lawn Cemetery.** If you enter the city via I-10, you'll have a perfect view of one of the wealthiest and newest area cemeteries. On foot, walk among elaborate individual grave sites and enormous marble family tombs encircled by cast-iron fencing and watched over by weeping stone angels. See p 23. ⓘ *90 min. 5100 Pontchartrain Blvd.* ☎ *504/486-6331. www.lakelawnmetairie.com. Free admission. Daily 9am–4pm. Closed holidays.*

Sometimes cabs are available on Canal Boulevard beside Cypress Grove and Greenwood cemeteries. Rather than take a chance, call a cab company such as United Cabs (☎ 504/522-9771) to arrange for a pickup beforehand at Lake Lawn Cemetery.

11 ★★★ **Mid City Lanes Rock 'n' Bowl.** You're guaranteed to pass a good time bowling (and drinking) to live music among locals of all ages and the occasional celebrity like Mick Jagger and Tom Cruise. ⓘ *90 min. 3000 S. Carrollton Ave.* ☎ *504/861-1700. www.rocknbowl.com. Tues–Sat 5–11pm.*

The Best **in Three Days**

1. St. Charles streetcar
2. Garden District
3. Still Perkin'
4. Lafayette Cemetery No. 1
5. Magazine Street
6. Audubon Zoo
7. Audubon Park

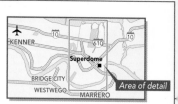

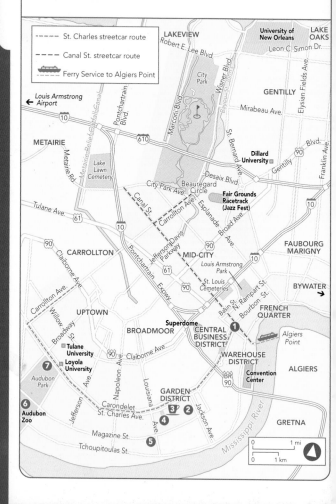

On your third day in New Orleans, I insist you get out of the Quarter. Many visitors miss out on the fabulous food, historic homes, and Southern hospitality found in other close-knit neighborhoods. The Garden District and Uptown both boast manicured mansions, sprawling live oak trees, colorful gardens year-round, eclectic restaurants, and boutique shopping along Magazine Street. After a day of exploring the city's greener side, you can return to the Quarter for more live music and revelry. START: **St. Charles streetcar at Canal and Carondelet streets.**

1 ★★★ kids **St. Charles Streetcar.** From 1835 to 1893, the St. Charles streetcar line was mule-driven. It went electric in the late 19th century. The present streetcars date from the 1920s and are listed on the National Register of Historic Places. If you have more than three people in your party and the streetcar isn't full, you can pull the back of one wooden bench so two benches face one another for a cozy tête-à-tête. ○ *30 min.–2 hr. Canal and Carondelet sts. or any stop along the route following St. Charles and Carrollton aves.* ☎ *504/827-8300. www.norta.com. $1.25 one-way fare.*

2 ★★ **Garden District.** You can opt for a guided walking tour or DIY; either way, you'll be transfixed by the exclusive estates and lush

gardens originally created by the nouveau riche who weren't welcome in Creole society. See the full Garden District neighborhood walk, p 54. ○ *90 min. Bounded by Magazine St. and St. Charles, Jackson, and Louisiana aves.*

3 **Still Perkin'.** Located among the Rink shops, this casual corner coffee spot is known for fresh bagels and unique spreads. *2727 Prytania St.* ☎ *504/899-0335. $.*

4 ★ **Lafayette Cemetery No. 1.** Despite its location in the Garden District, please do not venture into Lafayette on your own; only go with a tour group. This small historic cemetery is best known as the fictional resting place for Anne Rice's

A ride on the St. Charles streetcar should be on every visitor's to-do list.

Streetcar Dollars & Sense

Before you hop on the streetcar, note: A one-way fare is $1.25 (exact change required); a **JazzyPass** provides unlimited rides on streetcars or buses at a cost of $5 for 1 day, $12 for 3 days, or $20 for 5 days. Ask at your hotel or a tourist office for the nearest Jazzy-Pass vendor, or contact the **New Orleans Regional Transit Authority** (☎ 504/248-3900; www.norta.com).

beloved vampire Lestat; it was featured in the films *Interview with the Vampire* and *Double Jeopardy*. ⏱ *30 min. 1400 block of Washington Ave.* ☎ *504/525-3377. www.saveour cemeteries.org. Tour $10 adults, $5 children. Daily tour 10:30am. Closed some holidays.*

5 ★★ **Magazine Street.** Shopaholics could easily spend all day wandering along 6 miles (9.6km) of antiques shops, clothing and home-decor boutiques, art galleries, and restaurants. ⏱ *2–3 hr. Bookended by Canal St. and Audubon Park.*

6 kids **Audubon Zoo.** Though maybe not as flashy as younger zoos, the exhibits offer a glimpse at

many subtropical species that flourish in the city's heat and humidity. Kids will get a kick out of the underwater view of the silly sea lions. ⏱ *3 hr. 6500 Magazine St. See p 86.*

7 ★★★ kids **Audubon Park.** Watch wildlife from a bench along the lagoons or turn the kids loose on the playground. Other recreational activities include jogging, golf, tennis, and horseback riding. For more on Audubon Park, see p 84. ⏱ *45 min. 6500 St. Charles Ave. (across from Tulane and Loyola universities, btw. St. Charles Ave. & Magazine St.).* ☎ *504/581-4629. Daily 6am–10pm.* ●

The shops along Magazine Street.

Cemeteries: Cities of the Dead

1 Our Lady of Guadalupe Chapel and International Shrine of St. Jude
2 St. Louis Cemetery No. 1
3 St. Louis Cemetery No. 3
4 Terranova's Supermarket
5 Cypress Grove & Greenwood cemeteries
6 Lake Lawn Cemetery
7 Lafayette Cemetery No. 1

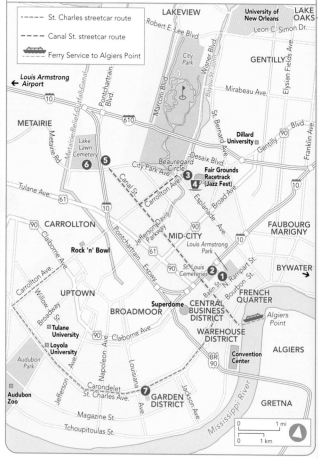

Previous page: A Mardi Gras Indian wears his handmade suit.

New Orleans's famous "Cities of the Dead" are both impressive and practical—it's impossible to have traditional underground graves when much of the city is below sea level. Their similarity to the famed Père-Lachaise cemetery in Paris, though, lends credence to some historians' insistence that the aboveground tombs were merely built in the French and Spanish tradition. In the 1990s, thieves regularly stole cemetery statues of angels and saints and other decorative pieces such as urns and wrought-iron fences to sell to antiques dealers around the world for big money. Local citizens and police have made a concerted effort to stop cemetery criminals, but it's a difficult task securing hundreds of thousands of graves and tombs throughout the city. Please be respectful of these sacred spaces. START: **Our Lady of Guadalupe Chapel, 411 N. Rampart St.**

❶ Our Lady of Guadalupe Chapel and International Shrine of St. Jude. The small chapel was built in 1826, preceding the more famous and grand St. Louis Cathedral by a good 25 years. Its initial purpose was to serve as a funeral church for the many victims of three yellow fever epidemics in the early 19th century. Today, many visitors travel a great distance to pray to Jude, patron saint of hopeless and impossible cases, as a last resort to heal terminal illness. ⏱ *20 min. 411 N. Rampart St.* ☎ *504/525-1551. www.judeshrine.com. Donations welcome. Gift shop Mon–Sat 9am–5pm. Masses daily starting at 7am.*

❷ ★★ St. Louis Cemetery No. 1. For your safety, please do not enter the city's oldest and most famous cemetery unless you're with a guided tour group. Opened in 1789 (most of the French Quarter burned the year before), the site is the resting place of such celebrated locals as the city's first mayor, Etienne de Boré; civil rights pioneer Homer Plessy; New Orleans's first African-American mayor, Ernest "Dutch" Morial; and world-champion chess player Paul Morphy. The most popular landmark is the Glapion family crypt, where revered (and feared) voodoo priestess Marie Laveau was supposedly laid to rest. To this day, followers mark her tomb with three small Xs, hoping she will grant them a wish. Needless to say, desecrating any tomb is rude. For more information on Marie Laveau, see the box "The Voodoo Queen of Bayou St. John"

The supposed tomb of Marie Laveau at St. Louis Cemetery No. 1.

on p 68. *① 1 hr. Basin Street Station Visitors Center, 501 Basin St. ☎ 504/525-3377. www.saveour cemeteries.org. Tour $20 adults, free children 12 and under. Mon–Sat 9am–3pm, Sun 9am–noon. Tours Sun 10am; Fri–Sat 1pm; meet at Basin Street station lobby. Closed holidays.*

Take the Canal Streetcar to City Park, then cross Bayou St. John to continue east on Esplanade Avenue.

❸ ★ **St. Louis Cemetery No. 3.** Imposing cast-iron gates usher you inside, where you'll find dramatic angel sculptures and elaborate aboveground tombs for some of the city's most distinguished Creole families. Established in 1854, the cemetery first opened 1 year after the city's worst yellow fever epidemic and began to fill quickly. Keep an eye out for tombs of prominent local figures such as legendary Storyville photographer Ernest Bellocq, missionary priest Father Adrian Rouquette, and free person of color and philanthropist Thomy Lafon (1810–1893), who willed $600,000 to various charities upon his death. One of the most

moving tributes can be found on the Gallier family tomb. Architect James Gallier, Jr., designed the cenotaph in memory of his Irish-born architect father, James Gallier, Sr., and his stepmother, Catherine Maria Robinson, who perished together when their steamship sank on its journey from New York to New Orleans on October 3, 1866. The cemetery is clean and well maintained because it continues to be active. In fact, there is a waiting list to buy burial space. *① 30 min. 3421 Esplanade Ave. ☎ 504/596-3050 or 504/482-5065. www.saveour cemeteries.org. Free admission. Mon–Sat 9am–3pm, Sun 9am–noon. Closed holidays.*

Walk back to City Park and take the Canal Streetcar to the cemeteries at the end of Canal.

❹ **Terranova's Supermarket.** Take a break from the dead and revive yourself with an ice cream, cold cuts, or other snacks at this family-run Italian grocery. For more on Terranova's, see p 64. *3308 Esplanade Ave. ☎ 504/482-4131. $.*

A gated tomb at Cypress Grove Cemetery.

Aboveground tombs at Lafayette Cemetery No. 1.

⑤ ★★ **Cypress Grove & Greenwood cemeteries.** After Cypress Grove Cemetery opened, bodies of volunteer firefighters were moved here from other cemeteries. Greenwood Cemetery is home to New Orleans's first Civil War memorial. Greenwood is also the final resting place of Pulitzer Prize–winning novelist John Kennedy Toole, who wrote A Confederacy of Dunces. See p 15. ⏱ *1–2 hr. 5200 Canal Blvd.*

⑥ ★ **Lake Lawn Cemetery.** This is New Orleans's most ornate and youngest cemetery, founded in 1872. It was originally an exclusive racetrack; rumor has it that Charles T. Howard, a "new money" Yankee, was denied membership there, so he exacted revenge by purchasing the property, demolishing the track, and opening this most opulent of graveyards. Howard's tomb is in the middle of the cemetery, along with more notable folks such as bandleader Louis Prima, Popeye's chicken founder Al Copeland, New Orleans district attorney Jim Garrison, and Anne Rice's husband, the poet Stan Rice. ⏱ *90 min. 5100 Pontchartrain Blvd.* ☎ *504/486-6331. www.lakelawnmetairie.com.*

Free admission. Daily 9am–4pm. Closed holidays.

Take bus route no. 27 Louisiana to the Garden District, exit at St. Charles and Louisiana avenues, go 5 blocks east then turn south on Washington Avenue.

⑦ ★★ **Lafayette Cemetery No. 1.** See p 17. ⏱ *1 hr. Entrance gate 1400 block Washington Ave.*

A sculpture in Lafayette Cemetery No. 1.

History Buffs

1. Jackson Square
2. Pontalba Buildings
3. The Presbytere
4. St. Louis Cathedral
5. The Cabildo
6. The Creole House and the Jackson House
7. Café du Monde
8. Madame John's Legacy
9. Miltenberger Houses (900 Royal St., 906 Royal St., and 910 Royal St.)
10. Lafitte's Blacksmith Shop Bar
11. Lalaurie Mansion
12. Croissant d'Or
13. Soniat House
14. Old Ursuline Convent

ⓘ Information

•-●-• Riverwalk streetcar route/stops

–•-• Vieux Carré loop route/stops

It could be argued that the entire city of New Orleans—which predates the founding of the U.S.A.—merits a spot on the National Register of Historic Places. But if your vacation days are limited, the French Quarter is rich with 18th- and 19th-century landmarks that have miraculously survived fires, floods, hurricanes, and modern development. START: **Jackson Square, bordered by St. Peter, Chartres, St. Ann, and Decatur streets.**

1 Jackson Square. Historically, Jackson Square has been a bustling social gathering place where you can shop, eat, and people-watch. See p 9. ⏱ *20 min. Bounded by Decatur, St. Ann, Chartres, and St. Peter sts. Free admission.*

2 Pontalba Buildings. These striking red-brick residences were constructed from 1849 to 1851 and were originally retail shops on the first floor and 16 high-end homes on the upper two and a half floors. (The half-floor attics were designated as the servants' quarters.) The ornamental ironwork inspired an architectural trend that can be seen throughout the Vieux Carré (French Quarter). It's a wonder that the residences were built at all. The developer, the Baroness Micaela Almonester de Pontalba, survived family feuding, divorce, and bullet wounds *before* embarking on this ambitious project, and tempestuous relationships with multiple architects and contractors *during*

the entire process. After the Civil War, the respectable tenants began to move out. By 1900, the homes had been divided into apartments crowded with the poor living in slum conditions. Despite restoration, most of the homes remain cut up into apartments, probably because they are in such demand. The Louisiana State Museum maintains one completely restored home, known as the 1850 House (523 St. Ann St.), which is open to the public. ⏱ *20 min. 523 St. Ann St. facing Jackson Square. ☎ 800/568-6968. www.crt.state.la.us/museum/properties/1850house.aspx. 1850 House admission $3 adults, $2 students/seniors, free children 12 and under. Tues–Sun 10am–4:30pm.*

3 The Presbytere. Originally known as the Casa Curial (Ecclesiastical House), the Presbytere was named for the Capuchin-monk residence, or presbytery, that once stood on its site. It was built in 1791 as a twin of the Cabildo, or Town

Painters, among other artists, line Jackson Square.

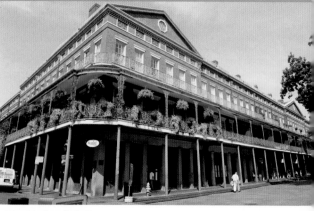

One of the Pontalba buildings on Jackson Square.

Hall, to the left of the cathedral. First it was used commercially, then it served as a courthouse until 1911, when it fell into the hands of the Louisiana State Museum. If your visit doesn't coincide with the Carnival season, you can get a taste of the revelry through the Presbytere's year-round Mardi Gras exhibit. The collection of ornate costumes and masks, rare artifacts, "royal baubles," music, and videos tell the story behind the holiday from its humble origins to its reputation today as one of the world's greatest parties. ① *1 hr. 751 Chartres St.* ☎ *800/568-6968. www.crt.state. la.us/museum/properties/presbytere.*

Elaborate Mardi Gras costumes on display at the Presbytere.

Admission $6 adults, $5 students/ seniors, free children 12 and under. Tues–Sun 10am–5:30pm.

④ **St. Louis Cathedral.** An iconic image of New Orleans, the 163-year-old church boasts ornate architecture and decor, including stained-glass windows and a massive mural. See p 10. ① *20 min. 615 Pere Antoine Alley (on Jackson Square).*

⑤ **The Cabildo.** The museum offers educational exhibits about early Louisiana history and culture, including mourning and burial customs, and the changing roles of women in the South. See p 10. ① *45 min. 701 Chartres St.*

⑥ **The Creole House and the Jackson House.** Architecturally, these homes fit right in with antebellum French Quarter residences and now house administrative offices for the Friends of the Cabildo. However, the site itself has seen quite a few changes over the past 3 centuries. In the early 19th century, there was a French guard house behind the *corps de garde,* or police station, where the Cabildo now sits. In 1769, during Spanish colonial times, a *calabozo,* or prison, replaced the guard house, though it, too, was

eventually demolished, in 1837.
⏱ 10 min. 616 Pirates Alley and 619 Pirates Alley. ☎ 800/568-6968 or 504/568-6968. www.crt.state.la.us. No public admission.

7 ★★★ kids Café du Monde.
Fuel up on strong café au lait (chicory coffee with milk) and melt-in-your-mouth beignets (pronounced ben-yays), fried doughnuts generously coated in powdered sugar. New Orleans's "original French Market coffee stand" started serving customers in 1862. *800 Decatur St.* ☎ *504/525-4544. $.*

8 Madame John's Legacy. The French Colonial style seems more in keeping with a plantation home on the bayou, but this simple two-story dwelling that sharply contrasts with its tall, elegant town-house neighbors is a survivor. Built in 1788 just after the great fire of that year, it is the second-oldest building in the Quarter after the Old Ursuline Convent. In fact, it is one of the few remaining examples of Creole buildings in the entire Mississippi Valley. The curious name alludes to a title character in New Orleans writer

You can't go wrong with a plate of beignets and a cup of chicory coffee at the Café du Monde.

George Washington Cable's short story, "Tite Poulette." Madame John was a quadroon (someone of one-quarter African ancestry) whose late lover willed this house to her. The Louisiana State Museum acquired the property and furnished the home with period pieces. ⏱ 30 min. *632 Dumaine St.* ☎ *800/568-6968 or 504/568-6968. www.crt.state.la.us/museum/online_exhibits/madam johnslegacy. Free admission. Tues–Sun 10am–4:30pm.*

9 Miltenberger Houses. Back in the day, it wasn't unusual for wealthy families to build homes for their offspring. But it's impressive that in 1838, widow and single

The Presbytere, below, and the Cabildo have nearly identical facades.

Madame John's Legacy.

mother Aimée Miltenberger managed to construct three separate residences, one for each of her sons, at a total cost of $29,176, then a lavish sum. The walls were made of imported red brick and the design—while mostly Creole—shows some Greek Revival influence, which was trendy at the time. For example, the staircase is indoors. Be sure to note the oak leaves with acorns in the cast-iron details, a symbol of food, shelter, health, and hospitality. ① *10 min. 900 Royal St., 906 Royal St., and 910 Royal St. No public admission.*

⑩ **Lafitte's Blacksmith Shop Bar.** Natives of New Orleans cringe at the thought of the Quarter becoming "Disneyfied," that is, prettied up so it looks like a pristine amusement park rather than real living history, with all of its quaint charms. The blacksmith shop bar's current cheesy look was a compromised

Lafitte's Blacksmith Shop Bar, a popular French Quarter watering hole.

"restoration" in response to criticism from the Vieux Carré Commission that the building was neglected. Now the tavern's halfhearted stucco job—allowing a few glimpses of the intriguing "brick-between-post" design—barely resembles the worn, but more evocative image that is still found on postcards and in books, making tourists wonder if it's even the same structure. Hard to believe that this is supposedly the oldest building in the Mississippi Valley, dating back to at least 1722. Named for infamous pirate Jean Lafitte, it attracted the literary likes of Tennessee Williams. ① *15 min. 941 Bourbon St. ☎ 504/593-9761. www.lafittesblacksmithshop.com. Free admission. Open Sun–Wed 10:00am–2am, Thurs–Sat 10am–4am.*

⑪ **The Lalaurie Mansion.** This is believed to be the most haunted house in the Quarter, which might be the reason why actor Nicolas Cage briefly owned it. In the early 1800s, a well-to-do Creole couple named Dr. Louis and Delphine Lalaurie resided here with a houseful of slaves. Delphine was known for extravagant parties, so when she was seen chasing a slave girl onto the roof who then fell to her death, neighbors chose to mind their own business. When a fire broke out in 1834, it was discovered that Madame Lalaurie had been slowly torturing to death some of her slaves, who were hidden away in secret rooms. Supposedly the cook, who was chained to her stove, started the fire, choosing death over her hell-on-earth existence. The Lalauries fled an angry mob and moved to Paris, never to be seen in New Orleans again. The home was restored, but subsequent occupants didn't stay long because they reported chilling screams and moans, strange occurrences, and, for a lucky few, ghost sightings. ① *5 min. 1140 Royal St. No public admission.*

The courtyard at the Old Ursuline Convent.

12 Croissant d'Or. In the early 1900s this was Angelo Brocato's bakery (which relocated to Mid-City) and had separate entrances for men and women. (You can still see the old ladies' entrance sign on the sidewalk.) The display case is filled with goodies, everything from chocolate and fruit-filled golden, flaky croissants to ham-and-cheese quiches. If you have a hard time choosing, keep in mind that the prices are low, so you can afford to pick a plateful, though the extra calories might cost you. Opt for a seat beside the decrepit fountain in the courtyard and toss a few crumbs to the friendly sparrows. *617 Ursulines St.* ☎ *504/524-4663. $.*

13 Soniat House. What is now a hotel was once the upscale Creole residence of wealthy plantation owner Joseph Soniat Dufossat. His father, chevalier Guy Saunhac du Fossat, was sent to Louisiana by Louis XV in 1751 to help the colonial governor defend against Native American attacks. Joseph built the house in 1829 and raised his family there until his death in 1852. By the time his wife died in 1865, the Quarter was no longer fashionable among aristocrats, and the house passed from owner to owner who cared little for its noble roots. In 1945, pioneering preservationists restored the home, and in 1983, it opened its doors as a hotel. The owners adored early-19th-century architecture and art and decorated the house with period furnishings. See p 146. ⏱ *10 min. 1133 Chartres St. Free admission. Open daily.*

14 Old Ursuline Convent. Once home to the first girls-only school in the U.S., the building now serves as a museum for local Catholic history dating back to 1718. ⏱ *40 min. See p 11. 1100 Chartres St.*

The old Angelo Brocato's sign outside the Croissant d'Or.

New Orleans Literati

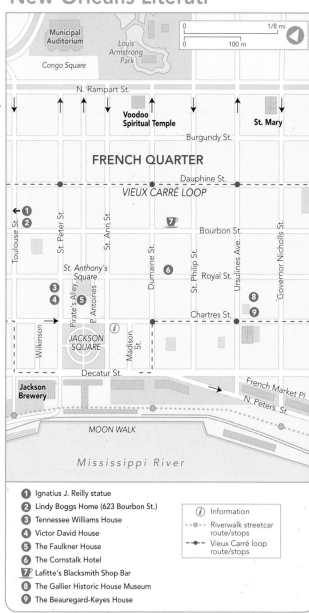

1 Ignatius J. Reilly statue
2 Lindy Boggs Home (623 Bourbon St.)
3 Tennessee Williams House
4 Victor David House
5 The Faulkner House
6 The Cornstalk Hotel
7 Lafitte's Blacksmith Shop Bar
8 The Gallier Historic House Museum
9 The Beauregard-Keyes House

(i) Information
•••○••• Riverwalk streetcar route/stops
--•--• Vieux Carré loop route/stops

If they weren't lucky enough to be born here, writers from William Faulkner to Richard Ford to Tennessee Williams have been drawn to New Orleans for its colorful history, eccentric characters, and sensual charms. Apparently, for writers, the city's contrasts—beauty and decay, rich and poor—kick-start the imagination. START: **Chateau Bourbon Hotel, 819 Canal St.**

1 Ignatius J. Reilly statue. At the Canal Street entrance to the Chateau Bourbon Hotel (see p 139) stands a likeness of Ignatius J. Reilly, the "hero" of John Kennedy O'Toole's novel *A Confederacy of Dunces.* The clock under which we first meet Reilly is now in the hotel's Clock Bar. *819 Canal St.*

2 Lindy Boggs Home. Truman Capote and Tennessee Williams both lived in this house (not at the same time). From the early 1970s until recently, it was home to

Victor David House.

former Congresswoman and Ambassador Lindy Boggs, a local political figure and the mother of national news personality Cokie Roberts. *623 Bourbon St. No public admission.*

3 Tennessee Williams House. If any work has ever captured the spirit of New Orleans, it's got to be Tennessee Williams's "A Streetcar Named Desire." He wrote the play from his attic room at 632 St. Peter's St. in 1946. Williams said that from this residence he heard "that rattle trap streetcar named Desire running along Royal and the one named Cemeteries running along Canal, and it seemed the perfect metaphor for the human condition. *632 St. Peter St. No public admission.*

4 Victor David House. In 1838 wealthy merchant Victor David built this exquisite example of sophisticated Greek Revival styling to show off his family's social standing. Nearly a century later, historian-novelist Grace King purchased the property to serve as headquarters for Le Petit Salon, of which she was president. The ladies' club was organized in 1924 in order to preserve New Orleans's, and in particular, the French Quarter's culture. *20 St. Peter St. No public admission.*

5 ★★★ The Faulkner House. From the 1920s to the '50s, the Vieux Carré was known as the "Greenwich Village of the South" for its steady influx of artists and

Books by William Faulkner on sale at Faulkner House Books.

Southern literature. The upper floors are private quarters for DeSalvo and James; a tour can be arranged in advance for a donation to their nonprofit organization, the Pirate's Alley Faulkner Society, Inc. Together with retired English professor Kenneth W. Holditch, the couple founded the society to assist writers and host events throughout the year, including the annual Words & Music arts festival in the fall. ① *30 min. 624 Pirate's Alley. Bookstore:* ☎ *504/524-2940. www.faulknerhouse.net or www. wordsandmusic.org. Free admission. Bookstore daily 10am–5:30pm. Closed Mardi Gras day.*

❻ **The Cornstalk Hotel.** Author Harriet Beecher Stowe is believed to have stayed here while researching local slave markets, which she featured in her famous anti-slavery novel *Uncle Tom's Cabin*. See p 52. ① *15 min. 915 Royal St. Free admission. Hotel open daily.*

❼ ★★ **Lafitte's Blacksmith Shop Bar.** Tennessee Williams liked to hang out here. With the candlelit bar, exposed antique brick, and rumored ghosts, it certainly invites creative musing. Order up your favorite drink and see where your mind takes you. See p 120. *941 Bourbon St.* ☎ *504/593-9761. $.*

writers attracted to the Quarter's decadent ways. Nobel Laureate William Faulkner was one of the bohemian literati, arriving in 1925 and renting a ground-floor apartment in this property. During his 1-year stay, he wrote his debut novel, *Soldiers' Pay*. Current owners Joseph DeSalvo, Jr., and Rosemary James painstakingly restored the Greek Revival–style Creole town house, built around 1840, which has since been named a national literary landmark. The ground floor is **Faulkner House Books,** where you can find a marvelous collection of

❽ **The Gallier Historic House Museum.** Designed and lived in by prolific local architect James Gallier,Jr. in the mid-1800s, it's allegedly the inspiration for vampires Lestat and Louis's home in Anne Rice's *Interview with the Vampire*. When constructed in 1857, the house was ahead of its time,

More Than Vampires

Anne Rice is New Orleans's most famous living native writer (and richest too, earning $7-million-plus per book). But you're missing out if you don't also read Pulitzer Prize–winning classics like John Kennedy Toole's *A Confederacy of Dunces* and Shirley Ann Grau's *The Keepers of the House*. The city's eccentric blue bloods are chronicled in Nancy Lemann's novel *Lives of the Saints*. If you plan to tour bayou country (see Lafitte in chapter 10), first pry open John Biguenet's *Oyster*. Uptown and the Audubon Zoo are the setting for Valerie Martin's *The Great Divorce*, in which a veterinarian faces the collapse of her marriage and the increasing divide between nature and man. For more suggestions, browse the book *The Booklover's Guide to New Orleans*, by former Times-Picayune critic Susan Larson.

featuring hot and cold running water, an indoor bathroom, and indoor kitchen. ⏲ *45 min. 1132 Royal St.* ☎ *504/525-5661. www. hgghh.org. Admission $10 adults, $8 seniors and children 8–18, free children 7 and under. Tours Mon,* *Thurs–Fri at 10am, noon, and 2pm; Sat at noon, 1pm, and 2pm.*

9 ★★ Beauregard-Keyes House & Garden. See p 11. ⏲ *30 min. 1113 Chartres St.*

Mardi Gras

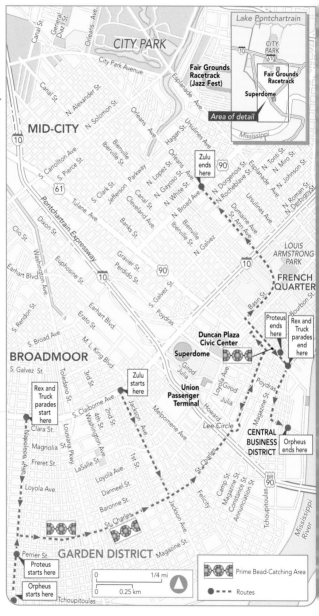

Mardi Gras—the biggest free party thrown in North America—always falls 46 days before Easter and is the city's most popular attraction. People love the crowds, costumes, and camaraderie; I don't know of another place or time where you can make so many friends just standing on a curb calling out for beads. Below are recommended parades for Lundi Gras (Mon) and Mardi Gras (Tues); citywide parades roll nearly every day in the 2 weeks prior to Mardi Gras day. START: **If you like raucous crowds, join the street party in the French Quarter, especially on Bourbon Street between the 500 and 1000 blocks. If you prefer a little more space, take a cab uptown near Napoleon Ave.**

A float from the Zulu Social Aid and Pleasure Club.

Lundi Gras Parades

❶ Proteus. The second-oldest Carnival krewe (Mardi Gras society) dates back to 1882 and comprises 275 men riding on about 20 old-fashioned floats that still use the original chassis from the 1880s. Throws include (plastic) pearls, lighted beads, flasks, and plush fish. *www.kreweofproteus.com. Starts uptown at Perrier St. and Napoleon Ave., turns east on St. Charles Ave., turns north on Canal St., makes a U-turn at Baronne St., and finishes at Canal and Chartres sts. Lundi Gras (Mon). Begins 5:15pm.*

❷ ★★★ Orpheus. Native New Orleanian Harry Connick, Jr.'s, young superkrewe recently celebrated its 20th anniversary (1993–2013) but boasts some of the most

Find a Parade

Arthur Hardy's Mardi Gras Guide is an annual magazine and my personal Mardi Gras bible come Twelfth Night (Jan 6, the official start of the Carnival season). It contains the all-important parade schedule, calendar of related events, and informative articles on Carnival history. You can buy one almost anywhere in the city—including bookstores, drugstores, and grocery stores (it usually comes out right after Christmas). You can also order a copy by phone ☎ **504/913-1563,** or online at www.arthurhardy.com.

A brass band leads revelers through the French Quarter on Mardi Gras Day.

popular megafloats, including the Leviathan and Trojan Horse. More than 1,200 men and women on 30 floats throw beads, pearls, silver doubloons, plush ducks, go-cups, and more. Celebrity guests serve as "royalty"; past guest monarchs include Whoopi Goldberg, Glenn Close, Sandra Bullock, Stevie Wonder, Quincy Jones, Laurence Fishburne, Vanessa Williams, Dan Aykroyd, James Brown, Little Richard, David Copperfield, Josh Hartnett, Anne Rice, Dominic Monaghan, and Brad Paisley. *www.krewe oforpheus.com. Starts uptown at Tchoupitoulas and Magazine sts. and ends downtown at the Convention Center. Lundi Gras (Mon). Begins 6pm.*

Mardi Gras Parades

❸ ★★ **Zulu.** Carnival's premier African-American parade was originally created as a parody of exclusive, haughty Rex before segregation ended; both krewes now allow anyone to join. As the 35 floats and 1,200 riders pass by, keep an eye out for prized Zulu coconuts, and hand-painted souvenirs that even the natives scramble for. Hang out near the cops keeping the crowds in check; Zulu members typically pass coconuts to them as thanks. Coconuts used to be thrown like beads, but must now be passed by hand for safety reasons. *www.kreweofzulu.com. Starts uptown at Jackson and St. Charles aves. and ends at Orleans Ave. and N. Broad St. Mardi Gras (Tues). Begins 8am.*

❹ ★★ **Rex.** The oldest parade debuted in 1872 and now has more than 600 men riding 27 floats. The royal costumes are a sight to behold—lots of gold and glitter.

Be sure to bring a costume if you plan on visiting New Orleans for Mardi Gras.

A crowd pleading and competing for "throws" from a passing float.

The throws are fairly traditional, including beads, pearls, doubloons, and go-cups. *www.rexorganization. com. Starts uptown at S. Claiborne and Napoleon aves. and ends downtown at Canal and St. Peter sts. Mardi Gras (Tues). Begins 10am.*

5 ★ kids **Truck parades.** Some parade watchers go home after the "official" end of Mardi Gras with the passing of Rex, but if you want more throws or just want the party to last, hang out to watch more than 200 themed truck floats decorated and ridden by family members. Kids often ride, too, and tend to throw stuffed animals and other cute trinkets to kids waving from the neutral ground or sidewalk. *Starts uptown at S. Claiborne and Napoleon aves. and ends downtown at Canal and St. Peter sts. Follows Rex.*

Beads Beget Beads

Want plenty of parade throws? At the very least, wear some "pearls" to the parade. Better yet, wear a costume and yell, "Throw me something, mister!" to show some Mardi Gras spirit. It's a given that float riders will always throw beads and stuffed animals to the kids on ladders; they're adorable and they stand out above the crowd, so if you're in the vicinity, you're guaranteed a neck full of beads too. If you and a neighboring reveler catch the same bunch of beads, it's common courtesy to share the strands.

Jazz History: Where the Greats Got Their Starts

1. Old U.S. Mint
2. New Orleans Jazz National Historic Park
3. Congo Square
4. 200–400 blocks of Loyola Avenue
5. Eagle Saloon
6. Iroquois Theater
7. Karnofsky Tailor Shop
8. Little Gem Saloon

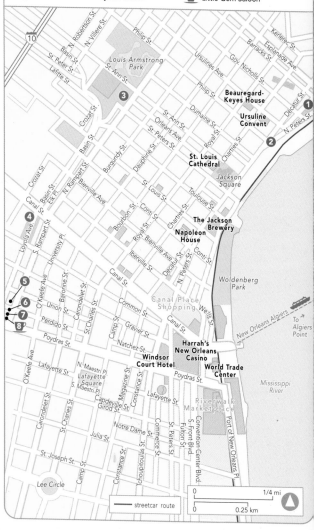

Many of jazz's greatest legends came from New Orleans. Walk along a few blocks of S. Rampart St., and you'll see the origins of some of New Orleans's most beloved and revered musicians. Stroll the French Quarter and you'll hear jazz wafting out the doorway of many a nightclub, bar, or retail store. This tour takes you through a section once known as the "Back of Town," along S. Rampart Street, which birthed such talents as Buddy Bolden, Louis Armstrong, and Jelly Roll Morton. Though some of the establishments on the tour below are closed and don't allow visitors, we still recommend taking a stroll through the neighborhoods where jazz originated and planted its still strong roots. START: **Canal streetcar, French Market Station.**

1 Old U.S. Mint. The Old U.S. Mint holds the sizable Louisiana State University Jazz Collection. In addition to such treasures as Louis Armstrong's cornet and bugle and Kid Ory's trombone, the exhibition holds tens of thousands of recordings, photographs, copies of sheet music, posters, and other jazz memorabilia. Though only a small amount (less than 1%) of the collection was damaged due to Hurricane Katrina and its aftermath, most of it was quickly refurbished. *400 Esplanade Ave.* ☎ *504/568-6968. http://lsm.crt.state. la.us/mintex.htm/. Admission $6 adults, $5 seniors and students, free children 12 and under. Tues–Sun 10am–4:30pm.*

2 ★★ New Orleans Jazz National Historical Park. The NOJNHP offers ranger-led walks, as well as provides self-guided walking tours, with opportunities to learn about New Orleans jazz music and native musicians.

You can download the tours online or stop by the visitors' center for a map. Documentary screenings and live music are also frequent; be sure to ask what's on tap while you're in town. The Oral History Project is a wonderful living document of New Orleans culture. Videotaped oral histories are available on more than 100 New Orleans legends (musical and otherwise) including Dooky Chase, Tuba Fats Lacen, Moon Landrieu, Willie Metcalf, Jr., and Babette Ory. The NOJNHP is in the process of moving and making Armstrong Park their permanent home. *Visitors Center: 916 N. Peters St.* ☎ *877/520-0677 or 504/589-4841. www.nps.gov/jazz. Tues–Sat 9am–5pm. Closed holidays. Headquarters: 419 Decatur St.* ☎ *504/589-4806. Mon–Fri 8am–4:30pm. Closed holidays.*

3 Congo Square. In the early 1800s slaves were allowed to gather in the

Palm Court Jazz Café.

Harry Connick, Jr. and Branford Marsalis take the stage at Jazz Fest.

square on Sundays for singing, dancing, and playing instruments (drums, in particular). Many musicians and musical styles grew from this cultural phenomenon. *In Louis Armstrong Park, N. Rampart St. btw. Toulouse and St. Phillip sts., facing the French Quarter.*

④ **200–400 blocks of Loyola Avenue.** Jelly Roll Morton and Louis Armstrong once lived along this section of Loyola Avenue. Also located here was Funky Butt Hall (formally known as Union Sons Hall), where Buddy Bolden would thrill the crowds with his one-of-a-kind cornet playing. These blocks now make up the New Orleans Civic Center. *200–400 blocks of Loyola Avenue.*

⑤ **Eagle Saloon.** Though it's in disrepair now, hopes run high for eventually turning this dilapidated structure into the New Orleans Music Hall of Fame. Jazz masters including Louis Armstrong, Buddy Bolden, Jelly Roll Morton, and King Oliver all played this dearly loved club that the Smithsonian recognized as the "birthplace of American jazz." One of three jazz-related venues in the building, the Eagle Saloon was a place for big names to relax between gigs at the next-door Odd Fellows and Masonic halls. *401 S. Rampart St. www.nomhf.org. No public admission.*

⑥ **Iroquois Theater.** Many jazz musicians got their start here by accompanying silent films and stage acts. A young Louis Armstrong is said to have won a talent contest here. *413–415 S. Rampart St.*

⑦ **Karnofsky Tailor Shop.** As a boy, Louis Armstrong worked here for the Karnofsky family. They took a shine to Louis and are rumored to have given him an advance on his pay so he could buy a cornet. Needless to say, their generosity paid off. Armstrong remained close to the family throughout his long career. The shop is listed in the National Register of Historic Places. *427–431 S. Rampart St.*

Jazz Clubs

Don't miss out on the best jazz around town. For complete reviews of these and other night spots, turn to our Nightlife chapter, on p 109.

Snug Harbor (p 120), 626 Frenchmen St.
Maison Bourbon (p 120), 641 Bourbon St.
Palm Court Jazz Café (p 120), 1204 Decatur St.
Preservation Hall (p 121), 726 St. Peter St.

Jazz Fest: Laissez les bon temps roulez!

What started as a local festival of jazz musicians has now become a world-renowned phenomenon featuring performances by the likes of Bruce Springsteen, Stevie Wonder, Bob Dylan, and Wynton Marsalis. The nearly weeklong **New Orleans Jazz & Heritage Festival** (the event's official name) is held at the Fair Grounds Race Course and celebrates the spirit and musical heritage of New Orleans. When the festival started it took place in Congo Square (see ❸, below) and attracted only a few hundred attendees. The festival now hosts hundreds of thousands of fans, so it's imperative to make your plans way ahead of time. Hotels, restaurant reservations, and flights can fill up months in advance. If possible, book up to a year out. You might not know who's on the bill yet, but you pretty much can't go wrong. Whether you're listening to an adored local blues band from the Delta or cheering on Harry Connick, Jr. or Dave Matthews, you're sure to pass a good time. For information, contact the New Orleans Jazz & Heritage Festival, 336 Camp St., Suite 250. ☎ 504/410-4100; www.nojazzfest.com.

8 Little Gem Saloon. Gulf oysters, salads, and cocktails should satisfy any hunger or thirst in your party. After suffering from neglect and dilapidation along with the other establishments listed above, the Little Gem Saloon was renovated as a jazz club and Southern soul food restaurant. It once housed a nightclub called Pete's Blue Heaven, where the Zulu Social Aid and Pleasure Club frequently started and ended its jazz funerals. *445 S. Rampart St. www.littlegem saloon.com.* ☎ *504/267-4863. $$*

Maison Bourbon.

Maison Bourbon in the French Quarter, an oasis of jazz in the Bourbon Street storm.

The Best Museums

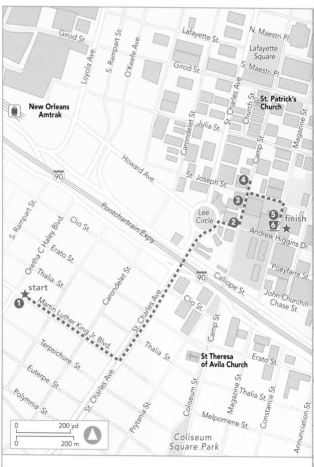

1. Southern Food and Beverage Museum & Museum of the American Cocktail
2. Civil War Museum at Confederate Memorial Hall
3. The Ogden Museum of Southern Art
4. Contemporary Arts Center
5. National World War II Museum
6. Soda Shop

Today's vibrant Arts District was once a shabby industrial area of abandoned warehouses. Thanks to adaptive reuse, these once-rundown buildings have been transformed into spacious galleries showcasing Southern art, history, and heritage. They have given new life—and unified purpose—to an old neighborhood. START: **St. Charles streetcar at Melpomene.**

A display of uniforms at the Civil War Museum at Confederate Memorial Hall Museum.

☎ 504/569-0405. www.southern food.org and www.museumofthe americancocktail.org. Check website for admission prices and hours.

❷ Civil War Museum at Confederate Memorial Hall. The oldest museum in Louisiana is absolutely worth a visit. Its Civil War memorabilia includes uniforms, photographs, guns, battle flags, swords, and personal belongings of Gen. Robert E. Lee, Gen. P. G. T. Beauregard, and Confederate president Jefferson Davis. ⏱ ½–1 hr. *929 Camp St.* ☎ *504/523-4522. www. confederatemuseum.com. Admission $8 adults, $5 children 7–14, free children 6 and under. Thurs–Sat 10am–4pm.*

Live music is on hand at the Ogden's annual White Linen Night.

❶ Southern Food and Beverage Museum & Museum of the American Cocktail. Moved to a new location in 2013, SOFAB documents the history of the area's famous foods and drinks. Rotating exhibits cover a wide spectrum of topics, ranging from White House cuisine to the history of greens (kale, collards, and the like) so often synonymous with Southern food. The Museum of the American Cocktail tells its own saucy story through artifacts, photos, and special exhibits dedicated to all types of spirits. ⏱ *1–2 hr. 1504 Oretha Castle Haley Blvd.*

3 ★★ **Ogden Museum of Southern Art.** Affiliated with the University of New Orleans, this young museum's permanent and rotating exhibitions are dedicated to Southern art in a variety of mediums—from clay and glass to paintings and photography—by self-taught and classically trained artists from 1890 to today. The sleek modern building is a soaring, inspiring space featuring a glass facade and "floating" staircase. ○ *1–2 hr. 925 Camp St.* ☎ *504/539-9600. www.ogdenmuseum.org. Admission $10 adults, $8 students/seniors, $5 children 5–17, free children 4 and under. Wed–Mon 10am–5pm, live music Thurs 6–8pm.*

4 **Contemporary Arts Center.** Modern art fans gather here to socialize and appreciate experimental plays, dance productions, concerts, and the occasional film screening. After walking through 10,000 square feet (929 sq. m) of gallery exhibits, unwind at the Cyber Bar & Café. ○ *1 hr. 900 Camp St.* ☎ *504/528-3800. www.cacno.org. Tickets $5 adults,*

$3 students/seniors. Wed–Mon 11am–5pm.

5 ★★★ **National World War II Museum.** A cavernous old warehouse has been transformed into an extraordinary tribute to the "Greatest Generation." The museum humanizes the soldiers no matter which side they fought on. My grandfather, a World War II veteran, spent 6 hours perusing the exhibits and artifacts, watching short documentaries, and talking to fellow veterans. ○ *2–3 hr. 945 Magazine St.* ☎ *504/527-6012 or 504/528-1944. www.nationalww2museum.org. Admission $18 adults, $14 students/seniors, $9 children 5–12, free children 4 and under. Daily 9am–5pm. Closed holidays.*

6 ★ **kids** **Soda Shop.** Award-winning chef John Besh puts his creative spin on American favorites like BBQ sliders and Bananas Foster milkshakes. Sandwiches, soups, and pastries are also good bets. *945 Magazine St.* ☎ *504/525-0522. $.* ●

The National World War II Museum.

The Upper French Quarter

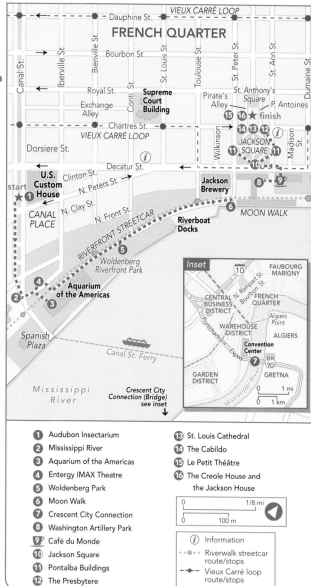

VIEUX CARRÉ LOOP

FRENCH QUARTER

Dauphine St.

Bourbon St.

Royal St.

Exchange Alley

Supreme Court Building

Pirate's Alley

St. Anthony's Square

P. Antoines

St. Peter St.

St. Ann St.

St. Louis St.

Toulouse St.

Conti

Bienville St.

Iberville St.

Canal St.

Dumaine St.

Chartres St.

VIEUX CARRÉ LOOP

Dorsiere St.

Decatur St.

Clinton St.

N. Peters St.

N. Clay St.

N. Front St.

U.S. Custom House

CANAL PLACE

start

Madison St.

Wilkinson

JACKSON SQUARE

finish

Jackson Brewery

MOON WALK

RIVERFRONT STREETCAR

Riverboat Docks

Woldenberg Riverfront Park

Aquarium of the Americas

Spanish Plaza

Mississippi River

Canal St. Ferry

Crescent City Connection (Bridge) see inset

Inset

10

CENTRAL BUSINESS DISTRICT

N. Rampart St.

Bourbon St.

FRENCH QUARTER

FAUBOURG MARIGNY

Pontchartrain Expwy.

WAREHOUSE DISTRICT

Algiers Point

ALGIERS

Convention Center

GARDEN DISTRICT

BR 90

GRETNA

Mississippi River

0 — 1 mi
0 — 1 km

1. Audubon Insectarium
2. Mississippi River
3. Aquarium of the Americas
4. Entergy IMAX Theatre
5. Woldenberg Park
6. Moon Walk
7. Crescent City Connection
8. Washington Artillery Park
9. Café du Monde
10. Jackson Square
11. Pontalba Buildings
12. The Presbytere
13. St. Louis Cathedral
14. The Cabildo
15. Le Petit Théâtre
16. The Creole House and the Jackson House

0 — 1/8 mi
0 — 100 m

(i) Information

•••••• Riverwalk streetcar route/stops

—•— Vieux Carré loop route/stops

Previous page: Ironwork balconies of the Miltenberger House.

The French Quarter is the lifeblood of New Orleans. Founded in 1718, the Vieux Carré (or Old Square, what we now call the French Quarter) comprised the original city of New Orleans. It burned twice—first in 1788, then again in 1794—and rebuilding took place during Spanish rule, which explains why much of the architecture reflects Spanish influence. The entire French Quarter is only 6 blocks wide by 13 blocks long, bordered by North Rampart Street, Esplanade Avenue, Canal Street, and the Mississippi River. The Upper Quarter is bounded by North Rampart, Orleans Street, Canal Street, and the Mississippi River. Hotels and souvenir shops dominate this area, so you'll find it to be busy and commercial, but many of the Vieux Carré's gems still anchor the neighborhood.

START: **Canal Street between Decatur and North Peters streets.**

1 kids **Audubon Insectarium.** Located in the former U.S. Customs House, this institution—featuring interactive exhibits with hundreds of thousands of insects—will thrill bug enthusiasts of all ages. Be sure to walk through the serene Butterfly Garden, home to hundreds of free-flying butterflies. 🕐 *1–2 hr. 423 Canal St.* ☎ *800/774-7394 or 504/581-4629. www.audubon institute.org. Admission $16.50 adults, $13 seniors, $12 children 2–12. Daily 10am–5pm.*

2 **Mississippi River.** Stroll along the parklike east bank of North

The Aquarium of the Americas is a great place to cool off and learn with the kids.

America's second longest river and the reason for New Orleans's existence. At this point, the mighty waterway measures 1 mile (1.6km) across and 200 feet (60m) deep. *At the end of Canal St.*

3 kids **Aquarium of the Americas.** One of the top five aquariums in the country features an enormous tank with a see-through tunnel from which you can view sea creatures on both sides and overhead, plus a tropical rainforest complete with waterfalls. Kids can pet baby sharks, see Spots the white alligator, and watch giant channel catfish. 🕐 *1–2 hr. 1 Canal St.* ☎ *800/774-7394 or 504/581-4629. www.auduboninstitute.org. Admission $22.50 adults, $17 seniors, $16 children 2–12. Daily 10am–5pm.*

4 kids **Entergy IMAX Theatre.** Large-screen 3-D documentaries on everything from dinosaurs to the Rolling Stones (was that redundant?) entertain kids of all ages. Be sure to inquire about aquarium/IMAX combination admission. 🕐 *1–2 hr. Next door to the aquarium.* ☎ *800/774-7394 or 504/581-4629. www.auduboninstitute.org. IMAX only tickets: $10.50 adults, $9.50 seniors, $8 children 2–12. Daily 10am–5pm.*

Looking over the Mississippi from Washington Artillery Park.

5 Woldenberg Park. Wander through nearly 20 acres (8 hectares) of open space along the riverfront and meditate on the elegant Holocaust Memorial designed by Israeli artist Yaacov Agam, a pioneer of kinetic art. *On the river behind the 500 block of Decatur St.*

6 Moon Walk. This scenic path is named for former New Orleans mayor Maurice Edwin "Moon" Landrieu, father of U.S. Senator Mary Landrieu (D-Louisiana) and Louisiana Lieutenant Governor Mitch Landrieu. Built in the 1970s, the wooden promenade encouraged the public use and appreciation for the riverfront after preservationists struck down a 1960s proposal for an expressway along the river. *Along the Mississippi River, btw. Canal St. and just past Orleans St.*

Entergy IMAX Theatre.

7 Crescent City Connection. The bridge comprises of two separate steel spans. The first was completed in 1958, the second in 1988. It ranks as the fifth most traveled toll bridge in the country, with an annual traffic volume of more than 63 million vehicles. *Spans the Mississippi River to Algiers Point.*

8 Washington Artillery Park. You get postcard-perfect views of Ol' Man River or Jackson Square depending on which direction you face. Sit on the amphitheater steps for people-watching and energetic dancing by tip-hustling street performers. *On Decatur St. next to Café du Monde.*

9 ★★★ kids Café du Monde. New Orleans's favorite coffeehouse has been around since 1862, when it debuted as a simple coffee stand in the French Market. It remains popular today among locals and tourists alike for its inexpensive signature beignets and café au lait. *800 Decatur St.* ☎ *504/525-4544. www.cafedumonde.com. $.*

10 Jackson Square. See p 9.

11 Pontalba Buildings. Despite an attempt on her life by her father-in-law, in which she was shot in the

chest and hands, and the acrimonious divorce that followed, the Baroness Micaela Almonester de Pontalba became a savvy businesswoman and designed and built these exclusive town homes in the 1840s. They remain in great demand today. See p 25. *St. Ann and St. Peter sts. facing Jackson Square.*

⓬ **The Presbytere.** True Mardi Gras fans can't resist the educational (and permanent) exhibit on the city's favorite holiday featured in the Presbytere. We've come a long way from mule-powered floats! See p 25. *751 Chartres St.*

⓭ **St. Louis Cathedral.** See p 10. *615 Pere Antoine Alley (on Jackson Square).*

⓮ **The Cabildo.** Step inside this national historic landmark and experience the sights, sounds, and stories of the birth of Louisiana. Originally a city council building, then a courthouse, this is the site of the Louisiana Purchase transfer ceremonies in 1803 as well as the infamous 1896 "separate but equal" Plessy v. Ferguson decision. *701 Chartres St. See p 10.*

The Presbytere houses a Mardi Gras Museum, which is part of the Louisiana State Museum.

⓯ **Le Petit Théâtre** is an early-20th-century Spanish Colonial–style building that serves one of the oldest community theater troupes in the country and hosts the annual Tennessee Williams Literary Festival every spring. See p 132. *616 St. Peter St.* ☎ *504/522-2081. www. lepetittheatre.com.*

⓰ **The Creole House and the Jackson House.** See p 26. *616 Pirates Alley and 619 Pirates Alley.*

A performance at Le Petit Théâtre in the French Quarter.

The Lower French Quarter

Congo Square | Louis Armstrong Park

N. Rampart St.

Voodoo Spiritual Temple

St. Mary

Burgundy St.

FRENCH QUARTER

Dauphine St.

VIEUX CARRÉ LOOP

St. Peter St.

St. Ann St.

Bourbon St.

Dumaine St.

Ursulines Ave.

Governor Nicholls St.

Barracks St.

start ★
St. Anthony's Square

finish ★

Pirate's Alley

P. Antoine's

Royal St.

Chartres St.

JACKSON SQUARE

Madison St.

St. Philip St.

Decatur St.

French Market Pl.

Jackson Brewery

N. Peters St.

MOON WALK

Mississippi River

0 — 1/8 mi
0 — 100 m

1 700–800 blocks of Royal Street
2 Dejan House
3 Madame John's Legacy
4 Miltenberger Houses
 (900 Royal St., 906 Royal St.,
 and 910 Royal St.)
5 The Cornstalk Hotel
6 Lafitte's Blacksmith Shop Bar
7 CC's Community Coffee House
8 The Lalaurie Mansion
9 The Gallier Historic House Museum
10 Clay House

11 Beauregard-Keyes House
12 Soniat House
13 Old Ursuline Convent
14 French Market
15 521 Gov. Nicholls St.
16 Old U.S. Mint
17 Gauche Mansion

ⓘ Information
••••• Riverwalk streetcar route/stops
–•– Vieux Carré loop route/stops

The Lower Quarter is more residential and less touristy. There are far fewer T-shirt and souvenir shops and many more condos, apartments, and single-family homes than you'll see in the Upper Quarter. A walk through the Lower Quarter will charm you with unique architecture and a sense of history. START: **Royal Street at Orleans Street.**

1 **700–800 blocks of Royal Street.** To walk Royal Street is to be surrounded by fine antiques, estate jewelry, home accessories, vintage paraphernalia, and more. By all means, don't limit yourself to this 2-block stretch if this is your cup of tea. Whenever I'm down this way, I stop by **Rodrigue Studio** (*730 Royal St.*), ground zero for Cajun artist George Rodrigue's famous "Blue Dog" paintings, **Hemmerling Gallery** (*733 Royal St.*), featuring works by the late folk artist Bill Hemmerling, and **Great Artists' Collective** (*815 Royal St.*), where you're guaranteed to find the perfect handcrafted souvenir. See the "The Best Shopping" chapter (p 73) for more details on individual stores.

2 **Dejan House.** The site was first purchased by city alderman Jean-Baptiste Dejan in 1813, well after the 1788 fire burned down everything on the block. He planned to build an impressive home for his family, as befit his station. But his ideas proved

Artifacts on display at Madame John's Legacy.

grander than his bank account; he lost the unfinished home to creditors in 1815. When the beautiful Creole town house was complete—from its elegant casement windows to its wrought-iron balcony railing—one of the creditors, merchant Nicholas Girod, purchased it outright. In the early 1900s, when much of the Quarter fell into ruin, the Dejan House was no exception. Thankfully, early Quarter preservationist Lilian Hovey-King acquired the property in 1944 and restored it so that we might enjoy it today. *824 Royal St. No public admission.*

The Dejan House.

3 Madame John's Legacy. See p 27. *632 Dumaine St.*

4 Miltenberger Houses. See p 27. *900, 906 & 910 Royal St.*

5 The Cornstalk Hotel. The unusual cornstalk cast-iron fence is one of only two in the city (the other can be found on the Garden District tour), although a cornstalk-and-sunflower fence guards the Dufour Plassan House in Esplanade Ridge. The owner of the original house on this site commissioned the fence for his homesick Midwestern wife. See p 32. *915 Royal St.*

6 Lafitte's Blacksmith Shop Bar. Supposedly the pirate Jean Lafitte and his brother Pierre posed as blacksmiths but used the shop (now a tavern) as a front for illegal activities. See p 120. *941 Bourbon St.*

7 CC's Community Coffee House. This is the South's retort to Starbucks, offering gourmet coffee, pastries, and sandwiches. Enjoy the view of lush balcony gardens across the street and the sound of carriage horses clop-clopping by. *941 Royal St.* ☎ *504/581-6996.* $.

8 The Lalaurie Mansion. This place attracts ghost hunters hoping to see or hear paranormal activity around what is rumored to be the most haunted house in the French Quarter. See p 28. *1140 Royal St.*

9 The Gallier Historic House Museum. The guided tour of this 1857 manse gives you insight into mid-19th-century life in New Orleans and owner-architect James Gallier's forward-thinking designs. See p 32. *1132 Royal St.*

10 Clay House. John Clay, the brother of American statesman Henry Clay, built this residence in 1828 for his wife. In the 1890s, Saint Frances Xavier Cabrini used it as a schoolhouse before moving to a larger campus at 3400 Esplanade Ave. to care for the large numbers of children orphaned by yellow fever. *618–620 Gov. Nicholls St.*

11 Beauregard-Keyes House & Garden. This lovely raised cottage and formal garden has survived nearly 200 years' worth of multiple owners, the mob, fire, hurricanes, and modern progress. *1113 Chartres St.*

12 Soniat House. What is now a hotel was once the Creole residence of wealthy plantation owner Joseph Soniat Dufossat. See p 146. *1133 Chartres St.*

The courtyard at the Beauregard-Keyes House.

A room at the Soniat House.

13 **Old Ursuline Convent.** See p 11. *1100 Chartres St.*

14 **French Market.** The bustling market has stood here since the 1700s. Unfortunately it's now more of a tourist trap (T-shirts anyone?) than anything else. Worth a look if you need some cheap souvenirs. *Decatur and N. Peters sts. from St. Ann to Barracks sts. www.french market.org. Open daily.*

15 **521 Gov. Nicholls St.** Actors Brad Pitt and Angelina Jolie purchased this stunning 1830s mansion soon after Hurricane Katrina, bringing much-needed hope and awareness to the city. Nearly 8,000 square feet (743 sq. m), it served as Cosimo Matassa's recording studio in the 1950s. All the musical legends of the time—including Fats Domino, Little Richard, Professor Longhair, and Allen Toussaint— recorded here. The house is believed to be haunted by the ghost of Professor Longhair. *521 Gov. Nicholls St. No public admission.*

16 **Old U.S. Mint.** Originally built in 1835 to mint money for both the United States and the Confederacy, this sturdy Greek Revival building now houses a fascinating jazz exhibit featuring priceless artifacts such as Louis Armstrong's first

trumpet. *400 Esplanade Ave.* ☎ *800/568-6968 or 504/568-6993. www.crt.state.la.us/museum/ properties/usmint*

17 **Gauche Mansion.** Frenchman John Gauche constructed this elegant, perfectly symmetrical two-story stucco home in 1856 at a cost of $11,000 and raised 12 children there. The granite Doric portico makes for an unusually understated entrance. Unlike most of the residences in the Quarter, the ornate ironwork was not added on later and is original to the home. *704 Esplanade Ave. (at Royal St.). No public admission.*

Typical New Orleans souvenirs for sale at the French Market.

Garden District

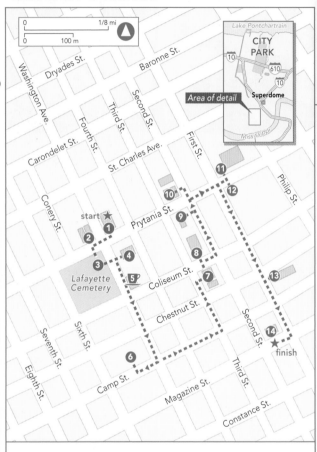

1/8 mi
100 m

Dryades St.
Baronne St.
Washington Ave.
Second St.
Third St.
Carondelet St.
Fourth St.
St. Charles Ave.
First St.
Conery St.
start ★
Prytania St.
Philip St.
Lafayette Cemetery
Coliseum St.
Chestnut St.
Seventh St.
Sixth St.
Camp St.
Eighth St.
Magazine St.
Second St.
Third St.
finish ★
Constance St.

Lake Pontchartrain
CITY PARK
Area of detail
Superdome
Mississippi

1. The Rink
2. 1500 Washington Ave.
3. Lafayette Cemetery No. 1
4. Colonel Short's Villa
5. Commander's Palace
6. Former site of Robb Mansion
7. Musson-Bell House
8. Robinson House
9. Davis House
10. Our Lady of Perpetual Help Chapel
11. Bradish Johnson House
12. Toby's Corner
13. Rosegate
14. Payne-Strachan House

Originally part of the city of Lafayette, the Garden District became a fashionable residential area for the nouveau riche who were not welcome among established wealthy Creole families in the French Quarter and Esplanade Ridge. Many of the 19th-century mansions have magnificent perfectly manicured gardens, hence the district's name. This exclusive neighborhood—bordered by Magazine Street and Jackson, St. Charles, and Louisiana avenues—is best experienced via the St. Charles streetcar and on foot. START: **Prytania Street at Washington Avenue.**

① **The Rink.** Originally a roller-skating rink built in 1884, this quaint little shopping center offers a coffee shop, bookstore, and boutiques. *2727 Prytania St.* ☎ *504/899-0335.*

② **1500 Washington Ave.** Now a private home, this is the former Behrman Gym, where 1892 World Heavyweight Champion boxer "Gentleman Jim" Corbett trained.

③ **Lafayette Cemetery No. 1.** Established in 1833 on the former Livaudais Plantation in the city of Lafayette, this cemetery is now located in one of New Orleans's most exclusive neighborhoods. Despite its location and small size, it's still not safe to visit alone. Please join a tour group. See p 17. *1400 block of Washington Ave.*

④ **Colonel Short's Villa.** Before you see the 1859 Italianate manse set back on the property, you'll be captivated by the unusual cornstalk

The renowned Commander's Palace.

cast-iron fence that surrounds it. (Similar fences are found guarding the Cornstalk Hotel in the French Quarter and the Dufour Plassan House in Esplanade Ridge.) *1448 Fourth St.*

Shops at the Rink.

The Robinson House, designed by architect Henry Howard.

5 Commander's Palace. Ordinarily, we'd recommend a snack stop here, but we're going to break our own rules. As long as you're in the Garden District, you might as well make the most of your time. If you're going to eat at one New Orleans restaurant, it should be Commander's Palace, the crown jewel in the Brennan family dining dynasty. See p 102. *1403 Washington Ave.* ☎ *504/899-8221. $$$.*

6 Former site of Robb Mansion. If you're wondering what these suburban-style brick ranch houses are doing in the middle of the tony Garden District, you're not the first to do so. Once an imposing private residence, then home to Newcomb College for Women, the property's original mansion fell into disrepair and was demolished in 1954. The lot was then subdivided for these modern dwellings. *1200 block of Washington Ave. (bordered by Chestnut, Camp & Sixth sts.).*

7 Musson-Bell House. Edgar Degas's French Creole uncle, Michel Musson, was one of the few non-Americans to live in this nouveau riche neighborhood. When he lost much of his wealth after the Civil War, he moved to a slightly less ostentatious mansion on Esplanade Avenue among Creole society. (Degas visited him there, and it is now known as the Degas House.) *1331 Third St.*

8 Robinson House. Architect Henry Howard created this extraordinary home for Walter Robinson, who moved from Virginia to New Orleans to become a cotton merchant, but instead went into his home state's best-known crop: tobacco. It took 6 years (1859–1865) to complete this massive home. Note the unusual curved portico; the roof was designed to collect rainwater and act as a cistern, thus pioneering indoor plumbing in the Garden District. *1415 Third St.*

9 Davis House. This gorgeous 1858 home belongs to the Women's Guild of the New Orleans Opera Association. It's one of the few area mansions available for special events. *2504 Prytania St.*

10 Our Lady of Perpetual Help Chapel. Originally built in 1858 as a private residence for wealthy merchant Henry Lonsdale, the home eventually served as a public chapel. Anne Rice attended Mass here as a girl and caused quite a stir when she purchased the property as an adult. The horror novelist never did quite fit in with her uptight old-money neighbors (and she appeared to prefer it that way). Actor Nicolas Cage subsequently owned the property. *2521 Prytania St.*

Payne-Strachan House.

⓫ **Bradish Johnson House.** This stunning French-Second-Empire home is now part of the Louise S. McGehee School for Girls. Local architect James Freret studied in Paris and classical influence can be seen in many of his homes and buildings. Sugar baron Bradish Johnson's ornate 1872 mansion cost $100,000—an outlandish sum at the time. *2343 Prytania St.*

⓬ **Toby's Corner.** Despite owner Thomas Toby's attempt to build a cottage in the Northern tradition, the Greek Revival–style cottage still employs the practical applications of local Creole architecture, such as being raised on brick piers for increased cooling. Built in 1838, this

is the oldest house in the Garden District. *2340 Prytania St.*

⓭ **Rosegate.** Anne Rice's former home was the first to be built on the block, in 1856. It serves as the setting for her *Witching Hour* series. Look for the delicate rosette pattern in the fence, which gave the Greek Revival town house its name. When Rice resided here, goth kids hung out on the street corner, waiting for her limo to show up so they could catch a glimpse of the famous horror novelist. *1239 First St.*

⓮ **Payne-Strachan House.** Built in 1849, this antebellum Greek Revival home is best known as the place where Jefferson Davis, president of the Confederacy, passed away in 1889 while visiting friends. *1134 First St.*

The raised brick piers underneath Toby's Corner allow for better cooling.

Uptown

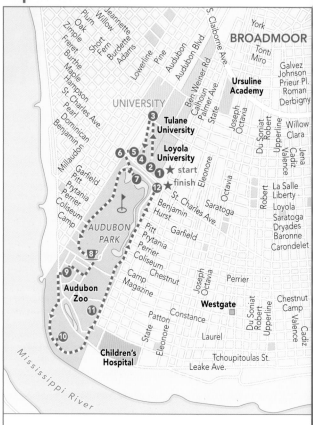

1 Loyola University
2 Holy Name of Jesus Church
3 Tulane University
4 Gibson Hall
5 Zemurray Mansion
6 Park View Guest House
7 Audubon Park
8 Audubon Café Clubhouse
9 Audubon Zoo
10 The Fly
11 Audubon Park Oak
12 Round Table Clubhouse

When I think of Uptown, I remember my first apartment, in a two-story Victorian home, and the freedom of being able to walk anywhere I needed to go. A little family grocery was around the block, Audubon Park was 10 minutes away on foot, and the St. Charles streetcar was easy to catch. No matter where you wander, you'll see historic mansions, giant live oak trees, and friendly faces. Bounded by the Mississippi River and Carrollton, Claiborne, and Jackson avenues, this is the largest neighborhood in the city.

START: **St. Charles Avenue between Loyola and Tulane universities.**

Loyola University.

1 Loyola University. Jesuits had a large role in shaping New Orleans, including introducing sugar cane to the region in the late 18th century.

In 1849 they opened the College of the Immaculate Conception downtown. The college grew, and in 1886 they purchased a "suburban" tract of land across from Audubon Park. Loyola College opened its doors in 1906 and was granted a university charter in 1912. Today the school serves more than 2,600 undergrads and nearly 2,000 graduate students. *6363 St. Charles Ave.* ☎ *800/456-9652 or 504/865-3240. www.loyno.edu.*

2 Holy Name of Jesus Church. In 1913, when the parish outgrew its little wooden chapel, construction began on this large church, which was completed in 1918. The carved-Carrara-marble altar alone cost $12,000. You can see the tall bell tower even from the far reaches of Audubon Park. Although the church still has its original 1892 bell, the ringing you'll hear is actually

Gibson Hall at Tulane University.

The Greek Revival–style columns of the Zemurray Mansion.

electric keyboard chimes, which, surprisingly, sound just as lovely. *6367 St. Charles Ave.* ☎ *504/865-7430. www.hnjchurch.org.*

❸ **Tulane University.** My alma mater was founded by seven doctors in 1834 as the Medical College of Louisiana. In 1884, thanks to a $1-million donation from Paul Tulane, it became Tulane University of Louisiana, a private nonsectarian school. The main campus moved to Uptown in 1894. Today it's the largest private employer in New Orleans. *6823 St. Charles Ave.* ☎ *504/865-5000. www.tulane.edu.*

❹ **Gibson Hall.** This massive neo-Romanesque structure, built in 1894, was the first to be constructed on the Uptown Tulane campus. *6823 St. Charles Ave.* ☎ *504/865-5000. www.tulane.edu.*

❺ **Zemurray Mansion.** Cotton broker and lumberman William T. Jay commissioned this formidable Greek Revival property in 1908, then sold it to fruit importer Samuel Zemurray in 1917. His widow bequeathed the mansion to Tulane University, and it's served as the Tulane president's residence ever since. *7000 St. Charles Ave.*

❻ **Park View Guest House.** This popular bed-and-breakfast was built as a boarding house in the late 1800s and is listed on the National Register of Historic Places. *7004 St. Charles Ave.* ☎ *888/533-0746 or 504/861-7564. www.parkviewguesthouse.com.*

❼ **kids Audubon Park.** Named for artist/ornithologist John James Audubon, who briefly lived in the New Orleans area, the 340-acre (136-hectare) park provides plenty of activities, from bird-watching to golf. See p 84. *6500 St. Charles Ave.*

The grand live oaks in Audubon Park.

On the porch at the Audubon Park Clubhouse.

(across from Tulane and Loyola universities, btw. St. Charles Ave. & Magazine St.). ☎ 504/581-4629.

8 Audubon Clubhouse Café. Head for a porch table so you can enjoy the park view while eating a sandwich at this casual cafe. The food is nothing to write home about, but it's convenient. *6500 Magazine St.* ☎ *504/212-5285. $.*

9 kids Audubon Zoo. In addition to your usual lions, tigers, and bears, the subtropical weather supports exhibits of exotic hot-climate animals, including the impressive 6- to 9-foot-long (1.8m–2.7m) Komodo dragons, averaging 200 pounds, from Indonesia. One of my favorite places is Monkey Hill, a man-made hill for New Orleans kids to contrast with the rest of the flat city. ⏱ *2–3 hr. See p 86. 6500 Magazine St.*

10 kids The Fly. Follow the curved road to the right of the zoo and you'll come to this riverside park. Locals nicknamed it "The Fly" because its shoreline is in the shape of a butterfly. It's fun to watch passing ships, tugboats, and tankers. *Riverview Dr. off Magazine St. btw. Audubon Zoo and the Mississippi River.*

11 Audubon Park Oak. After walking along the river, head back toward Magazine Street to see one of the city's largest live oaks. The trunk measures more than 35 feet (11m) around and the spread of the "crown" (overhead branches) is 165 feet (50m) across. *Btw. the Fly and Magazine St.*

12 Round Table Clubhouse. This charming historic home serves as headquarters to an exclusive men's social club organized in 1898. *6330 St. Charles Ave.*

Esplanade Ridge

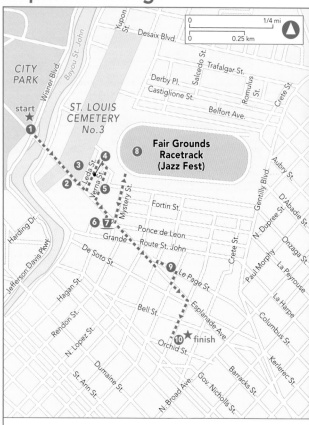

1. The General P.G.T. Beauregard Equestrian Statue
2. Old streetcar barn
3. St. Louis Cemetery No. 3
4. Luling Mansion
5. Verna Street bungalows
6. Terranova's Supermarket
7. Fair Grinds Coffee House
8. Fair Grounds Race Course
9. Cresson House
10. Dufour Plassan House

On Esplanade Avenue the sounds of city life are muffled by giant oak trees whose massive roots twist the sidewalks into roller coasters. The unmistakable squawk of bright-green monk parakeets adds to the exotic atmosphere. In the spring, confederate jasmine perfumes the entire neighborhood. In the summer, delicate crape myrtles are in full bloom. Block after block of imposing historic homes—from Victorians to raised villas—remind us that this was the Creole elite's enclave. START: **Esplanade Avenue at Wisner Boulevard, between City Park and Bayou St. John. Cross the bridge over the bayou and continue on Esplanade.**

1 The General P.G.T. Beauregard Equestrian Statue. This statue was completed in 1915 and is on the National Register of Historic Places. It's one of three monuments representing the "Cult of the Lost Cause," clung to by many Southerners after the Civil War. General Pierre Gustave Toutant Beauregard was one of three Confederate soldiers elevated to hero status in order to glorify what loyalists saw as a noble struggle. (Statues of Robert E. Lee and Jefferson Davis are also located in the city.) He lived lavishly in the French Quarter in the Beauregard-Keyes House. *Traffic circle at Esplanade Ave. and Wisner Blvd., directly across from main entrance to City Park.*

The P.G.T. Beauregard equestrian statue.

The Fair Grounds Race Course hosts hordes of visitors during Jazz Fest.

2 Old streetcar barn. This is one of the few surviving stations from the late 1800s for streetcars and the mules that pulled them. The New Orleans City Railroad Company began to convert to electricity in 1885 and gradually the mules were no longer needed. *Esplanade Ave. across from St. Louis Cemetery No. 3.*

3 St. Louis Cemetery No. 3. Home to wealthy Creole families in the mid to late 1800s, the cemetery remains active and well cared for. You can safely walk around without a tour group. See p 22. *3421 Esplanade Ave.*

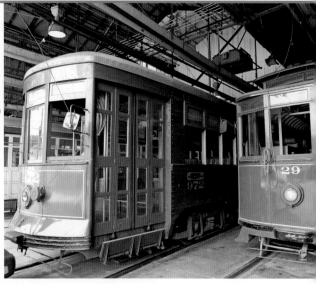

The Carrollton streetcar barn.

4 Luling Mansion. Originally a private residence, in 1871 it became the "Jockey Club" for the new Fair Grounds racetrack. Look for the cursive "L" on the concrete fenceposts. Though the building has been converted to apartments, the owner lives on-site and has painstakingly renovated it to its former glory. *1436 Leda Court.*

5 Verna Street bungalows. Bungalows were very popular in early-to mid-20th-century New Orleans, and this street has a few prime examples in rapid succession. At the corner of Marie and Verna streets, look for the gargoyle trumpet player with hair on fire keeping watch over the entry to a cozy bungalow *(1459 Verna St.).* Further down the block, you'll find an eye-catching bright purple bungalow with a rooftop deck *(1445 Verna St.).* Kitty-corner across the street is a stunning two-story bungalow featuring a vibrant color palette of violet, sunset orange, and olive green with complementary landscaping *(1432 Verna St.).*

6 Terranova's Supermarket. This place is a rarity these days: a small family-run grocery and convenience store. The third generation of Terranovas will help you find anything from a choice cut of meat to the best local hangouts. *3308 Esplanade Ave.* ☎ *504/482-4131. Mon–Fri 8am–6:30pm, Sat 9am–6:30pm. Closed Sun.*

7 Fair Grinds Coffee House. Painted tables and chairs, equally colorful locals, and strong iced coffee make for an eye-opening combination. Cash only. *3133 Ponce de Leon St.* ☎ *504/913-9073. $.*

8 Fair Grounds Race Course.
This is one of the oldest racetracks in the country, founded in 1872. The racing season runs from Thanksgiving Day to late March. It's also host to the famous New Orleans Jazz & Heritage Festival the last two weekends of April. See p 41. *1751 Gentilly Blvd.*

9 Cresson House. This grand and unique turreted Queen Anne was built in 1902. Note the dainty fleur-de-lis design on the heavy cast-iron gate. You can go farther down Esplanade, but I strongly recommend that you do not cross Broad Street on foot. Please be careful and alert at all times. *2809 Esplanade Ave.*

10 Dufour Plassan House. This 1870 mansion is relatively young compared to the historic houses you'll see on the bayou. In 1906, it

Inside Fair Grinds Coffee House.

was moved from Esplanade to its current location. The whimsically painted iron cornstalk-and-sunflower fence and old brick sidewalk add to its charms. *1206 N. White St.*

The bungalow at 1445 Verna St.

Bayou St. John

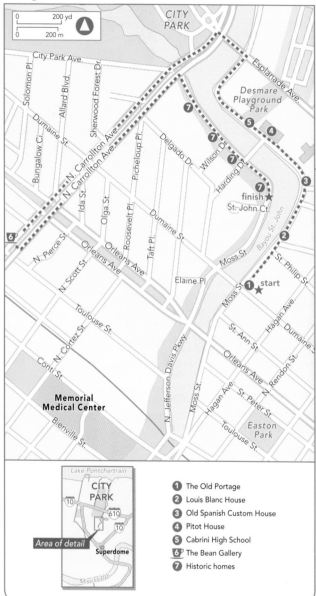

The Old Portage
Louis Blanc House
Old Spanish Custom House
Pitot House
Cabrini High School
The Bean Gallery
Historic homes

Once a busy waterway used by Native Americans, Bayou St. John now offers a sleepy respite from urban life. You may either follow the sidewalk for a close-up view of the cottages, shotgun houses (a house laid out in such a straight line that you could shoot a shotgun through the front door and the ammo would go straight out the back door), and Greek Revival homes, or scramble down the small grassy levee to the edge of the water and look for fish, turtles, frogs, and ducks. When you cross Grand Route St. John, you're standing on the oldest street in New Orleans, originally a Native American portage between the bayou and the Mississippi River. In 1699 the Biloxi Indians guided French Louisiana colonists and brothers Pierre Le Moyne d'Iberville and Jean-Baptiste Le Moyne de Bienville through what is now Grand Route St. John. START: **Take Canal streetcar to Jefferson Davis Parkway stop, then head northeast to beginning of bayou.**

1 The Old Portage. From this historic landmark on the bayou side of the street you can spot turtles, pelicans (on occasion), jumping fish, little diving birds, cranes, egrets, and ducks. Ellen Barkin was filmed jogging along the bayou for the 1987 movie *The Big Easy* costarring Dennis Quaid. ○ *10 min. On the bayou side of the intersection of Moss and Bell sts.*

2 Louis Blanc House. One of the oldest homes on the bayou (predating the Louisiana Purchase of 1803) is on shady Moss Street, named for the Spanish moss hanging from the live oaks bordering the bayou. ○ *10 min. 924 Moss St.*

3 Old Spanish Custom House. Believed to be the oldest surviving residence in New Orleans, this elegant two-story, West Indies–style plantation home was built in 1784 and sold for just over $1 million at auction in 2009. Hundreds of people took advantage of the public open house in the days leading up to the auction, eager to satiate their curiosity about the nearly 3,000-square-foot (279-sq.-m) colonial mansion. It's unknown whether the buyer, Lyndon Saia, who grew up in the neighborhood, will maintain it as a private residence or

Louis Blanc House.

open it to the public. At one time, it overlooked flatboat traffic from Lake Pontchartrain to the French Quarter via the bayou to a man-made canal built in the 19th century by Spanish Governor Carondelet that was filled in more than 50 years ago. The only boats you'll see these days are canoes and the occasional rowboat. ○ *10 min. 1300 Moss St. at Grand Route St. John.*

The wide galleries on the Pitot House are typical of West Indies–style architecture.

4 Pitot House. This house was built around 1799 for James Pitot, the first mayor of incorporated New Orleans. This is an excellent example of a West Indies–style plantation home, featuring wide galleries, large rounded columns, and a weathered wooden fence. In 1962 a proposed expansion of the neighboring high school threatened its existence. The Louisiana Landmarks Society moved the house a block away to save it from the wrecking ball. *1440 Moss St.*

5 Cabrini High School. Young girls whose parents succumbed to yellow fever found sanctuary in the orphanage with its founder, Frances Xavier Cabrini (she was canonized in 1946). By 1959 there was no longer a need for the orphanage, and the sisters opened Cabrini Catholic High School for girls. The campus extends back behind Esplanade to a two-story complex built around 1965 on Moss Street overlooking Bayou St. John. Personal and group tours of the shrine, chapel, and/or school are available to individuals, schools, and church groups by calling the campus minister at ☎ 504/483-8690. ⏱ *15–45 min. Back of campus 1400 Moss St. overlooking Bayou St. John; original school entrance, 3400 Esplanade Ave. Free admission. Tours by appointment only.*

The Voodoo Queen of Bayou St. John

Voodoo in New Orleans is a unique combination of beliefs borrowed from African animism, Haitian spirit faiths, and Roman Catholicism. The latter was likely incorporated to placate the local authorities. Even so, the city's European population feared voodoo and its practitioners. In fact, in the late 18th century, Spanish governor Bernardo de Gálvez wouldn't allow slaves from Martinique into the territory because he believed that their devotion to voodoo made them dangerous. Police raids in the French Quarter became common enough that voodoo practitioners went out to the "country" along Bayou St. John. Priestess Marie Laveau (1801–1881), a free woman of color, was particularly influential. She made good use of her connections with servants throughout the city and knew secrets about the elite that were attributed to black magic but were most likely due to spying, blackmail, and her early career as a hairstylist to the wealthy. Nevertheless, she drew thousands of believers to the "Wishing Spot" on the bayou. They supposedly drank the blood of roosters and danced with snakes, the earthly symbol of the voodoo god.

The Old Spanish Custom House may be the oldest surviving residence in New Orleans.

Cross the bridge over the bayou. Cross Carrollton Avenue, then head southwest a couple blocks to the intersection of Carrollton Avenue and St. Peter Street.

6️⃣ The Bean Gallery. The strong Turkish coffee will give you a much-needed boost. Choose from fresh pastries and healthy sandwiches to fuel up for more walking. *637 N. Carrollton Ave.* ☎ *504/324-8176. $.*

Cross Carrollton Avenue again, head northeast for a block or two, then turn right on West Moss Street so you can explore the southwest side of Bayou St. John.

7️⃣ Historic homes. Whether you choose to follow the sidewalk for a closer look or view them from across the street along the bayou, you'll see block after block of cottage, Colonial, Victorian, Greek Revival, and shotgun homes. The different styles serve as a veritable timeline of when they were built. As the city's drainage system improved, there was more

residential development, particularly by the wealthy in search of a country home. Feel free to turn right on Harding Drive, which will intersect again with Moss Street after a few blocks. 🕐 *30 min. 800–1500 blocks of West Moss St.*

An assortment of goodies on offer at the Bean Gallery.

Carrollton

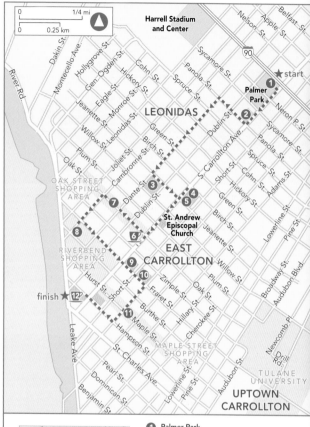

1. Palmer Park
2. Nix-Arensman House
3. Carrollton Streetcar Barn
4. Weston Ward House
5. Sully-Wormuth-Langfels House
6. Rue de la Course
7. 8100–8500 blocks Oak Street shopping
8. The Riverbend shopping
9. Wilkinson House
10. D'Antoni House
11. 7500–8000 blocks Maple Street browsing
12. Camellia Grill

Area of detail

Carrollton is nestled into a bend in the Mississippi River nearly 6 miles (9.7km) from the Quarter via the St. Charles streetcar. Incorporated as the city of Carrollton in 1833, the city of New Orleans annexed it in 1874. The main thoroughfare is Carrollton Avenue, which is shaded by massive oaks, like its more famous cousin, St. Charles Avenue. It's a very walkable neighborhood, with plenty of coffeehouses and shopping on Oak and Maple streets and in the Riverbend. START: **End of the St. Charles streetcar line at S. Carrollton and S. Claiborne avenues.**

1 Palmer Park. Among the large live oaks are a World War II memorial and a plaque commemorating the City of New Orleans annexing the Town of Carrollton in 1874. *Bounded by Carrollton and Claiborne aves., and Dublin and Sycamore sts.*

2 Nix-Arensman House. Though it appears much younger, this eclectic Arts and Crafts–style brick home was built in 1915. Both brick and stone are used for the battered columns, an unusual feature. *2140 S. Carrollton Ave., at Sycamore Place, southeast corner of Palmer Park.*

3 Carrollton Streetcar Barn. Peek inside to see the St. Charles line streetcars get repaired or prepped for their leisurely route. If you follow the tracks, you'll understand why no off-street parking is allowed for the residents of the streets bordering the barn. Be doubly careful when you cross the street! *Half-block off Carrollton Ave., btw. Jeannette, Dublin, and Willow sts.*

Italianate detail on the Weston Ward House.

4 Weston Ward House. This lemon-yellow Victorian home dates from the late 19th century and features delicate Italianate details. *1537 S. Carrollton Ave.*

The Arts and Crafts–style Nix-Arensman House.

5 Sully-Wormuth-Langfels House. Locally renowned architect Thomas Sully designed and built this 1893 home—a stunning combination of Queen Anne and Colonial Revival elements—as his office and personal residence. *1531 S. Carrollton Ave.*

6 Rue de la Course. Step inside this converted early-19th-century bank building for European-style coffee and pastries. The sandwiches are okay; you're better off with a warm almond croissant. *1140 S. Carrollton Ave.* ☎ *504/861-4343. $.*

7 8100–8500 blocks Oak Street shopping. After a rough couple of decades, this unique main street is flourishing once again, offering antiques, clothing, books, jewelry, cafes, bars, and more. *Btw. Carrollton Ave. and Leonidas St.*

8 The Riverbend shopping. Independent boutiques like the women's clothing shop Yvonne La Fleur (*8131 Hampson St.* ☎ *504/866-9666*) and familiar commercial chain stores now occupy the former site of a 19th-century public open market. Go behind the mini strip mall to find a tiny park, restaurants, and shops located in renovated Victorian homes. *Bounded by Carrollton and Leake aves. and Maple St.*

9 Wilkinson House. This striking and rare Tudor Gothic home was built by Englishman Nathaniel Wilkinson in 1849. The mansion and its manicured lawn and gardens cover half a city block. *1015 S. Carrollton Ave.*

10 D'Antoni House. If you like the Prairie style, you'll love this massive brick villa built by Edward Sport in 1917. Note the complementary garage and intricately detailed iron fence surrounding the sprawling property. *7929 Freret St.*

11 7500–8000 Maple Street browsing. Around here you'll find a mix of cute Victorian shotgun homes and cottages among restaurants and small businesses, including local hangouts PJ's Coffee & Tea. *(7624 Maple St.* ☎ *504/861-5335) and Maple Street Book Shop (7529 Maple St.* ☎ *504/866-4916).*

12 Camellia Grill. Ask for a slice of fried pecan pie and wash it down with a thick vanilla shake. *626 S. Carrollton Ave.* ☎ *504/309-2679. $.* ●

Camellia Grill is known for their delicious pecan pie.

Shopping Best Bets

Best **T-Shirt Designs**
Dirty Coast, *5631 Magazine St. and
329 Julia St. (p 79)*

Best **Shoe Store**
★★ Feet First, *4122 Magazine St.
and 526 Royal St. (p 79)*

Best **Art-Supply Store**
National Art & Hobby,
5835 Magazine St. (p 78)

Best **Home Furnishings**
★★★ Loisel Vintage Modern,
2855 Magazine St. (p 81)

Best **Wood Furniture**
Shaun Wilkerson Handcrafted
Furniture, *3023 Chartres St. (p 81)*

Best **Fine Lingerie**
★★ House of Lounge,
2044 Magazine St. (p 79)

Biggest **Collection of Cajun &
Jazz Music**
★★★ Louisiana Music Factory,
210 Decatur St. (p 82)

Best **Gallery**
★ A Gallery for Fine Photography,
241 Chartres St. (p 80)

Best **Department Store**
Saks Fifth Avenue, *301 Canal St.
(p 80)*

Best **Hip & Wearable
Women's Fashion**
Trashy Diva, *829 Chartres St. and
2048 Magazine St. (p 79)*

Best **Day Spa**
★★ Woodhouse Day Spa, *4030
Canal St. (p 77)*

Best **Vintage Clothing**
Le Garage, *1234 Decatur St. (p 79)*

Best **Place for Antiques**
Keil's Antiques, *325 Royal St. (p 77)*

Best **Wine Store**
Martin Wine Cellar,
3500 Magazine St. (p 80)

Best **Chocolates**
★ Blue Frog Chocolates,
05707 Magazine St. (p 80)

Best **Pralines**
Southern Candymakers,
334 Decatur St. (p 80)

Best **Museum Shop**
★★ National World War II
Museum, *945 Magazine St. (p 81)*

Best **Secondhand Book Shop**
★ Beckham's Bookshop,
228 Decatur St. (p 79)

Best **Modern Book Shop**
★★★ Octavia Books,
513 Octavia St. (p 79)

Best **Record Store**
Domino Sound, *2557 Bayou Rd.
(p 81)*

Previous page: An impressive display of toys on sale at the Idea Factory.

Royal Street Shopping

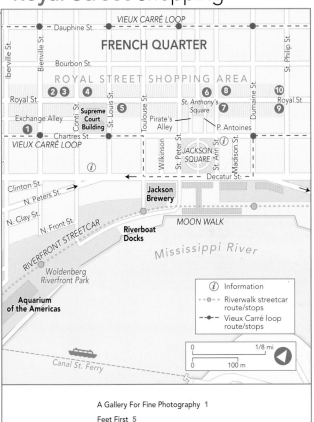

A Gallery For Fine Photography 1

Feet First 5

Great Artists' Collective 8

Hemmerling Gallery 6

Ida Manheim Antiques 4

The Idea Factory 9

Keil's Antiques 3

Rodrigue Studios 7

Rothschild's Antiques 2

Sigle's Antiques & Metalcraft 10

Magazine Street Shopping

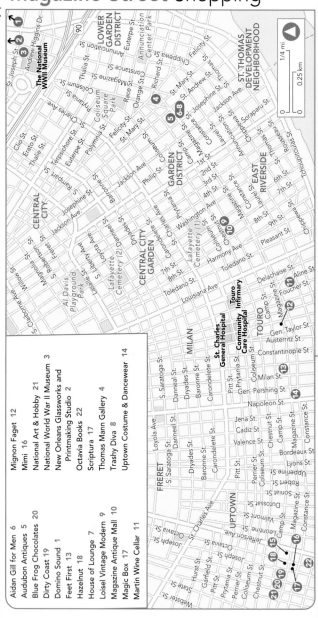

Aidan Gill for Men 6
Audubon Antiques 5
Blue Frog Chocolates 20
Dirty Coast 19
Domino Sound 1
Feet First 13
Hazelnut 18
House of Lounge 7
Loisel Vintage Modern 9
Magazine Antique Mall 10
Magic Box 17
Martin Wine Cellar 11

Mignon Faget 12
Mimi 16
National Art & Hobby 21
National World War II Museum 3
New Orleans Glassworks and
Printmaking Studio 2
Octavia Books 22
Scriptura 17
Thomas Mann Gallery 4
Trashy Diva 8
Uptown Costume & Dancewear 14

French Quarter Shopping

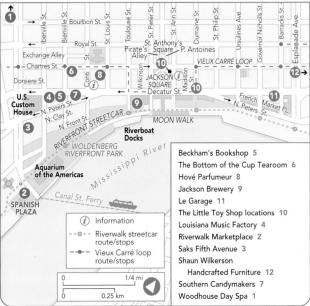

Beckham's Bookshop 5
The Bottom of the Cup Tearoom 6
Hové Parfumeur 8
Jackson Brewery 9
Le Garage 11
The Little Toy Shop locations 10
Louisiana Music Factory 4
Riverwalk Marketplace 2
Saks Fifth Avenue 3
Shaun Wilkerson
    Handcrafted Furniture 12
Southern Candymakers 7
Woodhouse Day Spa 1

Shopping A to Z

Antiques

Audubon Antiques MAGAZINE
STREET This two-story treasure
stocks everything from curios to
authentic antiques. *2025 Magazine
St.* ☎ *504/581-5704. AE, MC, V.
Map p 76.*

Ida Manheim Antiques ROYAL
STREET Proprietor Ida Manheim's
grandfather started the business in
1919 in this same location. She continues the family tradition of Conti-
nental, English, and Oriental
furnishings, along with porcelain,
jade, silver, and fine paintings.
409 Royal St. ☎ *504/620-4114 or
888/627-5969. www.idamanheim
antiques.com. AE, DISC, MC, V. Map
p 75.*

Keil's Antiques ROYAL
STREET Established in 1899 and
run by Peter Moss, great-grandson
of the founder, Keil's has a consid-
erable collection of 18th-and
19th-century French and English
furniture, chandeliers, and jewelry.
325 Royal St. ☎ *504/522-4552.
www.keilsantiques.com. AE, MC, V.
Map p 75.*

Magazine Antique Mall MAGA-
ZINE STREET Twenty-eight independent dealers show off their
wares, including 18th- and 19th-
century furnishings, music boxes,
dollhouse miniatures, porcelain,
and antique toys. *3017 Magazine St.*
☎ *504/896-9994. AE, MC, V. Map
p 76.*

Ida Manheim Antiques.

Rothschild's Antiques ROYAL STREET   This fourth-generation-run antiques store and full-service jeweler will have you fantasizing about a home makeover in no time. *321 Royal St.* ☎ *504/523-5816. MC, V. Map p 75.*

Sigle's Antiques & Metalcraft ROYAL STREET   Sigle's specializes in delicate ironwork, like you've seen in the French Quarter. Stop in here and take home a unique souvenir. *935 Royal St.* ☎ *504/522-7647. MC, V. Map p 75.*

Art Supplies
National Art & Hobby MAGA-ZINE STREET   Get creative with everything from crafts to paintbrushes to scrapbooking supplies. *5835 Magazine St.* ☎ *504/899-4491. MC, V. Map p 76.*

Beauty Products & Cosmetics
Aidan Gill for Men MAGAZINE STREET/CENTRAL BUSINESS DISTRICT   In addition to luxury soaps and handmade shaving accessories, Irish proprietor Aidan Gill and staff offer hairstyling and "The Shave at the End of the Galaxy," an old-fashioned hot-towel shave. *2026 Magazine St.* ☎ *504/587-9090 and 550 Fulton St.* ☎ *504/566-4903. www.aidangillformen.com. AE, MC, V. Map p 76.*

Hové Parfumeur CHARTRES STREET   For more than 75 years, the family-run Hové has created original perfumes, colognes, body oils, lotions, and soaps. They currently offer 53 original fragrances, including the popular Tea Olive, Vetivert, and

Hové Parfumeur has a scent for just about everyone.

Creole Days. *434 Chartres St.*
☎ *504/525-7827. www.hove
parfumeur.com. AE, DISC, MC, V.
Map p 77.*

Books & Stationery
★★ Beckham's Bookshop
FRENCH QUARTER Browse thousands of rare and used books in a cozy atmosphere. How can you not love a place where both dogs and beer are welcome? *228 Decatur St.*
☎ *504/522-9875. www.beckhams
bookshop.com. Map p 77.*

★★★ Octavia Books UPTOWN
Husband-and-wife proprietors Tom Lowenburg and Judith Lafitte renovated this 100-year-old former grocery into a modern yet inviting bookstore where you can wander among the stacks or lounge on the outdoor patio and listen to the waterfall cascade into a small goldfish-stocked pond. *513 Octavia St.*
☎ *504/899-READ [7323]. www.
octaviabooks.com. MC, V. Map p 76.*

Scriptura MAGAZINE STREET
Wordsmiths will love this full-service upscale stationer, which sells custom invitations, engraved and embossed stationery, leather journals, address books, desk accessories, wine journals, photo albums, and fine writing instruments.
5423 Magazine St. ☎ *504/897-1555.
www.scriptura.com. AE, MC, V. Map
p 76.*

Clothing & Shoes
★ Dirty Coast MAGAZINE
STREET If your friends are only going to get a T-shirt as a souvenir, tell them to skip the raunchy offerings on Bourbon Street in favor of these creative and clever tees.
5631 Magazine St. ☎ *504/324-3745.
www.dirtycoast.com. A, MC, V. Map
p 76.*

★★ Feet First ROYAL STREET/
MAGAZINE STREET Shoes, handbags, and accessories galore, with new inventory added every week. The crowded shelves feature more than 50 designers—from Michael Kors to Kate Spade—plus local favorites Dirty Coast, NOLA Couture, and Feelgoodz. *4122 Magazine
St.* ☎ *504/899-6800, and 526 Royal
St.* ☎ *504/569-0005. www.feetfirst
stores.com. AE, DISC, MC, V. Map
p 75 and p 76.*

★★ House of Lounge MAGAZINE STREET All you need to know is that the real Erin Brockovich spent lots of money here on designer lingerie and loungewear.
2044 Magazine St. ☎ *504/671-8300.
www.houseoflounge.com. MC, V.
Map p 76.*

Le Garage DECATUR STREET
On offer is an ever-changing selection of retro and vintage clothing.*1234 Decatur St.* ☎ *504/522-
6639. MC, V. Map p 77.*

Mimi MAGAZINE STREET Model the latest fashions and accessories from this upscale boutique.
5500 Magazine St. ☎ *504/269-
6464. www.miminola.com. AE, MC,
V. Map p 76.*

Trashy Diva MAGAZINE STREET
Designer-owner Candice Gwinn brings glamour back with her ultra-feminine vintage-inspired dresses, blouses, jackets, and lingerie.
829 Chartres St. ☎ *504/581-4555,
and 2048 Magazine St.* ☎ *888/818-
DIVA or 504/299-8777. www.trashy
diva.com. AE, MC, V. Map p 76.*

Uptown Costume & Dancewear MAGAZINE STREET If you like to play dress up, this is the place for you; lots of hats, wigs, makeup, and masks to help your transformation. *4326 Magazine St.* ☎ *504/895-7969. www.uptown costume.com. AE, MC, V. Map p 76.*

Department Store

Saks Fifth Avenue FRENCH QUARTER The upscale store offers designer clothing, shoe and handbag collections galore, plus jewelry, housewares, fine beauty products, and more. *The Shops at Canal Place, 301 Canal St.* ☎ *504/524-2200. www.saksfifthavenue.com. AE, DISC, MC, V. Map p 77.*

Food, Chocolates & Wine

★ **Blue Frog Chocolates** MAGAZINE STREET It's impossible to resist Fancy's "Sin in a Tin" toffees or delectable French truffles, so go ahead, indulge. *5707 Magazine St.* ☎ *504/269-5707. www.blue frogchocolates.com. MC, V. Map p 76.*

Martin Wine Cellar MAGAZINE STREET Browse an impressive array of wines, spirits, and champagnes, plus preserves, coffee, tea, crackers, cookies, and cheese. *3500 Magazine St.* ☎ *888/407-7496 or 504/894-7420. www.martinwine.com. AE, DISC, MC, V. Map p 76.*

★★ **Southern Candymakers** DECATUR STREET Satisfy your sweet tooth with Mississippi Mud squares, alligator- and crawfish-shaped chocolates, caramel turtles, sugar-coated pecans, and hand-dipped ice cream, among other delights. *334 Decatur St.* ☎ *504/523-5544 or 800/344-9773. www. southerncandymakers.com. AE, MC, V. Map p 77.*

Galleries

★ **A Gallery for Fine Photography** FRENCH QUARTER Even if you can't afford an original 19th-century print, it's worth stepping inside to view the extensive

photo collections with a focus on Southern artists and subjects. *241 Chartres St.* ☎ *504/568-1313. www. agallery.com. AE, MC, V. Map p 75.*

Great Artists' Collective ROYAL STREET More than 40 local artists combine their talents to offer a multi-medium gallery, from ceramics and glasswork to paintings and photographs. *815 Royal St.* ☎ *800/621-6179 or 504/525-8190. www.greatartistscollective.com. Map p 75.*

Hemmerling Gallery ROYAL STREET Originally from Chicago, the late Bill Hemmerling lived the last decades of his life immersed in Louisiana culture in the small town of Ponchatoula. His works reflect the spiritual creativity of the region. *733 Royal St.* ☎ *504/524-0909. www.hemmerlingart.com. Map p 75.*

New Orleans Glassworks and Printmaking Studio MAGAZINE STREET With New Orleans's infamous heat and humidity, this is the last place where you'd expect a glassworks studio, complete with 800-pound furnace. Their demonstrations are very cool. *727 Magazine St.* ☎ *504/529-7279. www. neworleansglassworks.com. AE, MC, V. Map p 76.*

George Rodrigue is most famous for his "Blue Dog" paintings.

Hazelnut on Magazine Street.

Rodrigue Studios ROYAL STREET
What does it say about art appreciation that artist George Rodrigue toiled in obscurity painting dark, moody, and critically acclaimed Cajun landscapes, but found fame and fortune when he started painting his beloved late dog in bright blue? If you're not familiar with the critically panned but publicly embraced Blue Dog icon, do come in. *730 Royal St.* ☎ *504/581-4244. www.georgerodrigue.com. AE, MC, V. Map p 75.*

Gift Shops
The Bottom of the Cup Tearoom CHARTRES STREET
Opened in 1927 and supposedly the oldest tearoom in the U.S., here you can browse holistic books, jewelry, tarot cards, crystals, and healing wands. *327 Chartres St.* ☎ *800/729-7148 or 504/524-1997. www.bottomofthecup.com. MC, V. Map p 77.*

★★ National World War II Museum MAGAZINE STREET
Features World War II–themed books, clothing, model airplanes, watches, and more. *945 Magazine St.* ☎ *504/528-1944. www.national ww2museum.org. MC, V. Map p 76.*

Housewares, Furnishings & Art
Hazelnut MAGAZINE STREET
Stop in for elegant home furnishings, including decorative

accessories and glassware, plus unusual New Orleans–themed gifts. *Mad Men*'s Bryan Batt is a native New Orleanian and part owner. *5515 Magazine St.* ☎ *504/891-2424. www.hazelnutneworleans.com. MC, V. Map p 76.*

Loisel Vintage Modern MAGAZINE STREET   Browse through an eclectic mix of vintage and modern home furnishings, including lighting and artworks. *2855 Magazine St.* ☎ *504/899-2444. www.loiselvintage modern.com. A, MC, V. Map p 76.*

Shaun Wilkerson Handcrafted Furniture FRENCH QUARTER
Artist-owner Shaun Wilkerson's award-winning custom furniture designs are influenced by 19th-century New Orleans architecture. *3023 Chartres St.* ☎ *504/208-7998. www.shaunwilkerson.com. MC, V. Map p 77.*

Jewelry
Mignon Faget MAGAZINE STREET   Local artist Mignon Faget creates fine jewelry inspired by nature and Louisiana icons. *3801 Magazine St.* ☎ *504/891-2005 or 800/375-7557. www.mignonfaget. com. MC, V. Map p 76.*

Thomas Mann Gallery MAGAZINE STREET   Artist-proprietor Thomas Mann designs "techno-romantic" jewelry (you'll know it when you see it) and carries contemporary furniture. *1810 Magazine St.* ☎ *504/581-2111. www.thomas mann.com. MC, V. Map p 76.*

Music
★★★ Domino Sound MID CITY
You can easily pass an hour or two going through the comprehensive vinyl collection that goes beyond rock and roll. *2557 Bayou Road.* ☎ *504/309-0871. No credit cards. Map p 76.*

★★★ Louisiana Music Factory

DECATUR STREET Overwhelmed by the wealth of regional music on display? Just ask a knowledgeable staff member (this ain't Best Buy!) to help you select the best Cajun, zydeco, R & B, jazz, blues, and gospel. *210 Decatur St.* ☎ *504/586-1094. www.louisianamusic factory.com. AE, MC, V. Map p 77.*

The sign outside Louisiana Music Factory.

Shopping Centers

Jackson Brewery FRENCH QUARTER The old "Jax" brewery is now a complex of shops with a variety of offerings such as Cajun and Creole food, clothing, and souvenirs. *600 Decatur St.* ☎ *504/566-7245. www.jacksonbrewery.com. AE, MC, V. Map p 77.*

Riverwalk Marketplace FRENCH QUARTER A covered mall running along the river from Poydras Street to the Convention Center, this is a popular venue that's surprisingly scenic. **NOTE:** Renovations are currently under way, with the mall planning to reopen in 2014 as The Outlet Collection at Riverwalk. *500 Port of New Orleans Place.* ☎ *504/522-1555. www.riverwalkmarketplace. com. AE, MC, V. Map p 77.*

Toys

★★ The Idea Factory

ROYAL STREET There's no cheap plastic stuff at this shop that offers old-fashioned wooden toys like alphabet and number blocks, trains, and pull toys. *924 Royal St.* ☎ *800/524-IDEA or 504/524-5195. www.ideafactory neworleans.com. MC, V. Map p 75.*

Little Toy Shop FRENCH QUARTER An extra-special kids' shop, offering a spectrum of goods from unique dolls to wooden toys to miniature cars and trucks. *513 St. Ann St.* ☎ *504/523-1770 and 900 Decatur St.* ☎ *504/522-6588. AE, MC, V. Map p 77.*

Magic Box MAGAZINE STREET This specialty toy store featuring the latest and greatest as well as nostalgic favorites has something for kids of all ages. *5508 Magazine St.* ☎ *504/899-0117. www. magicboxneworleans.com. AE, MC, V. Map p 76.* ●

Audubon Park

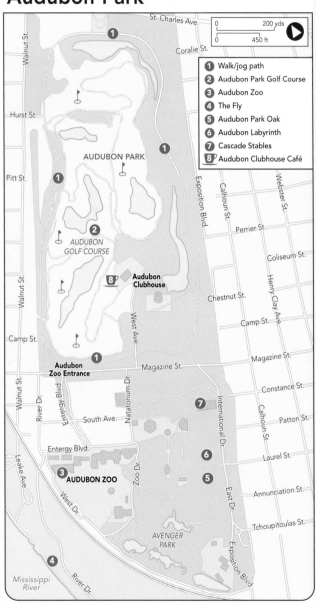

St. Charles Ave.

Coralie St.

| 0 | 200 yds |
| 0 | 450 ft |

1 Walk/jog path
2 Audubon Park Golf Course
3 Audubon Zoo
4 The Fly
5 Audubon Park Oak
6 Audubon Labyrinth
7 Cascade Stables
8 Audubon Clubhouse Café

Walnut St.

Hurst St.

AUDUBON PARK

Pitt St.

Exposition Blvd.

Calhoun St.

Webster St.

Perrier St.

Coliseum St.

AUDUBON GOLF COURSE

Henry Clay Ave.

Chestnut St.

Camp St.

Walnut St.

Audubon Clubhouse

West Ave.

Magazine St.

Camp St.

Audubon Zoo Entrance

Magazine St.

Constance St.

Patton St.

River Dr.

Entergy Blvd.

Natatorium Dr.

South Ave.

International Dr.

Calhoun St.

Entergy Blvd.

Laurel St.

AUDUBON ZOO

Zoo Dr.

Annunciation St.

Leake Ave.

West Dr.

East Dr.

AVENGER PARK

Tchoupitoulas St.

Exposition Blvd.

Mississippi River

River Dr.

Previous page: Audubon Park.

Audubon Zoo

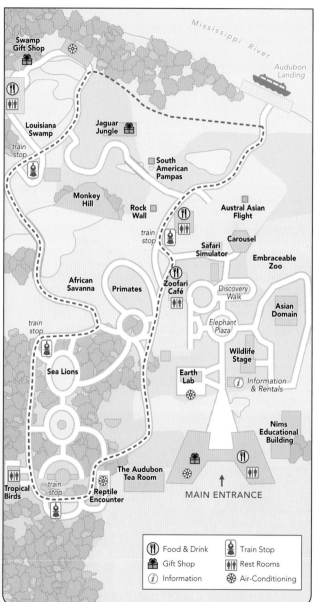

Mississippi River

Audubon Landing

Swamp Gift Shop

Louisiana Swamp

train stop

Jaguar Jungle

South American Pampas

Monkey Hill

Rock Wall

Austral Asian Flight

train stop

Safari Simulator

Carousel

Embraceable Zoo

African Savanna

Primates

Zoofari Café

Discovery Walk

Asian Domain

train stop

Elephant Plaza

Sea Lions

Wildlife Stage

Earth Lab

i Information & Rentals

Nims Educational Building

Tropical Birds

train stop

The Audubon Tea Room

Reptile Encounter

MAIN ENTRANCE

🍴	Food & Drink	🚶	Train Stop
🎁	Gift Shop	🚻	Rest Rooms
i	Information	❄	Air-Conditioning

A s a college student and Uptown resident, I often sought quiet refuge in Audubon Park. The 340-acre (136-hectare) public park (which is privately owned by the Audubon Institute) was named after famed French-American naturalist and painter John James Audubon. (His mother was a French/Spanish Creole from Louisiana, and he created much of his art in the pelican state.) This parcel of land was originally set aside to be a park in 1879, hosted the World's Fair in 1884, and officially opened as Audubon Park in 1886 with master-plan renovations by renowned park designer Frederick Law Olmsted in 1897. One of the World's Fair buildings, the 30-acre (12-hectare) Horticulture Hall, remained in use until a hurricane destroyed it in 1915. On the southern end of the park, live oaks, lagoons, gardens, and fountains offer a peaceful respite from urban hustle and bustle. As you go north, you'll discover recreational opportunities such as golf, swimming, tennis, and the acclaimed Audubon Zoo. START: **6500 St. Charles Avenue, across from Tulane and Loyola universities.**

❶ **Walk/jog paths.** Follow the nearly 2-mile (3.2km) asphalt track shaded by centuries-old live oak trees dripping with Spanish moss and enjoy colorful year-round landscaping and dreamy lagoons filled with birds, turtles, and fish. ⏲ *1 hr. Open daily sunrise–sunset.*

❷ **Audubon Park Golf Course.** *Golf Digest* named it the best golf course over a hundred years old in the country (though one has to wonder how many century-old golf

courses there are in the U.S.). Reserve your tee time by phone, at the Pro Shop, or online. ⏲ *2–4 hr. 6500 Magazine St. (btw. Walnut & Calhoun sts.).* ☎ *504/861-2537. www.audoboninstitute.org/golf. Open Mon 10am–sunset, Tues–Sun 7am–sunset.*

❸ **kids Audubon Zoo.** I recommend you go early or late if you want to see the animals active in the outdoor exhibits; the midday sun keeps them denned up and out

Enjoy a quiet stroll in Audubon Park.

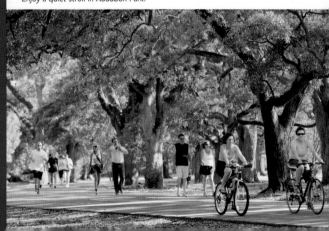

The entrance to the Audubon Zoo.

of sight. Plan to eat before or after your visit, as the food is expensive and just okay. ⏱ *2–3 hr. 6500 Magazine St.* ☎ *800/774-7394 or 504/ 581-4629. www.auduboninstitute. org/visit/zoo. Admission $17.50 adults, $13 seniors, $12 children 2–12. Add $5 for Cool Zoo access. Mon–Fri 10am–5pm, Sat–Sun 10am–6pm.*

④ **The Fly.** This small Riverside Park is popular with locals for picnics, ball games, and watching boat and barge traffic down the Mississippi. *River Road off Magazine St., along the Mississippi River.*

⑤ **kids Audubon Park Oak.** Measuring more than 35 feet (11m) around and 165 feet (50m) across its crown, you'll want to try a group hug touching hands. ⏱ *15 min. Btw. the Fly and Magazine St.*

⑥ **kids Audubon Labyrinth.** Unlike a maze where there are dead ends, a labyrinth offers many different paths, none of which are wrong. Simply follow the stone path's twists and turns until you arrive at the center, then return to the outer circle. ⏱ *20 min. East Dr. at Laurel St.* ☎ *504/304-4427. www.labyrinthataudubonpark.org. Free admission. Open daily sunrise–sunset.*

⑦ **kids Cascade Stables.** Your guide will take you on a 45-minute horseback ride around the perimeter of the park. The steeds are always friendly and eager to go for a ride; children ages 8 and up are welcome to saddle up. ⏱ *1 hr.* ☎ *504/891-2246. www.cascade stables.net. $40 per trail ride. Reservations preferred. Fri Noon–4pm; Sat–Sun 10am–4pm.*

⑧ **Audubon Clubhouse Café.** A convenient stop for sandwiches and a gorgeous park view. *6500 Magazine St.* ☎ *504/212-5285. $.*

A gorilla at the Audubon Zoo.

City Park

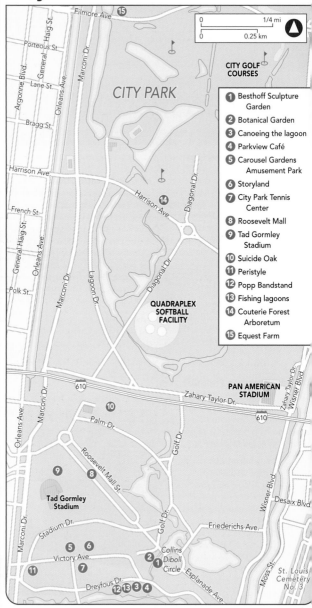

	0	1/4 mi
	0	0.25 km

CITY GOLF COURSES

CITY PARK

QUADRAPLEX SOFTBALL FACILITY

PAN AMERICAN STADIUM

Tad Gormley Stadium

1 Besthoff Sculpture Garden
2 Botanical Garden
3 Canoeing the lagoon
4 Parkview Café
5 Carousel Gardens Amusement Park
6 Storyland
7 City Park Tennis Center
8 Roosevelt Mall
9 Tad Gormley Stadium
10 Suicide Oak
11 Peristyle
12 Popp Bandstand
13 Fishing lagoons
14 Couterie Forest Arboretum
15 Equest Farm

At 1,300 acres (520 hectares), City Park is the fifth largest urban park in the U.S. The 150-year-old city oasis lost many of its mature live oaks—some more than 400 years old—in Hurricane Katrina. When the floodwaters had receded, it was discovered that all of the grass, flowers, and bushes had died, coated in brown muck. A grass-roots effort by local citizens helped the park reblossom and again offer golf, tennis, horseback riding, walking trails, and kids' activities, all surrounded by the natural beauty of giant trees, lagoons, and wildlife. START: **1 Palm Drive, bounded by City Park Avenue and Canal, Robert E. Lee, and Wisner boulevards.**

① kids Besthoff Sculpture Garden. The 5-acre (2-hectare) garden contrasts a backdrop of moss-draped lives oaks with the clean lines of contemporary sculpture. My favorite pieces are Rona Pondick's haunting stainless-steel *Monkeys*, George Segal's *Four Lines Oblique*, for its simplicity and graceful motion, and Jean-Michel Othoniel's whimsical *Tree of Necklaces.* The Besthoffs commissioned the latter, which are giant glass bead necklaces suspended from live-oak branches, evoking the plastic beads caught in trees lining a Mardi Gras parade route. Kids will love Louise Bourgeois's huge bronze spider, but please, no climbing! ① *1 hr. 1 Dueling Oaks Dr., adjacent to the New Orleans Museum of Art.* ☎ *504/658-4100. www.noma.org. Free admission. Mon–Fri 10am– 4:45pm, Sat–Sun 10am–5pm.*

Figures in the Besthoff Sculpture Garden.

② New Orleans Botanical Garden. Hurricane Katrina flooding wiped out the garden's entire collection of orchids, staghorn ferns, bromeliads, and many more carefully cultivated plant species and old-growth trees. This was a devastating blow to one of the few remaining public gardens designed by the WPA in the 1930s. Thanks to dedicated staff and volunteers, the 12 acres (4.8 hectares) of Art Deco– era gardens, fountains, ponds, and sculptures, plus a horticultural library, are again open and thriving. The Historic Train Garden is an extraordinary and unique model of the City of New Orleans. As you follow the walkway, you'll see tiny streetcars and trains just like the ones that dutifully traveled the city from the late 1800s to the early 1900s. Each structure is made entirely out of botanical materials, including home models organized by neighborhood. ① *1 hr. 3 Victory Ave.* ☎ *504/483-9386. www.new orleanscitypark.com/botanical- garden. Admission $6 adults, $3 children 5–12, free 4 and under. Tues– Sun 10am–4:30pm.*

③ kids Canoe the Lagoon. Take a relaxing ride in a pedal boat or canoe and explore up to 8 miles (13km) of lagoons. You'll see swans, ducks, geese, turtles, frogs, and fish. ① *1 hr. City Park Big Lake at Esplanade Ave.* ☎ *504/224-2601. Boat rental $10/per person per*

The Best of the Outdoors

half-hour. Nov–Feb Sat–Sun 11am–5pm.; Mar–Oct Sat–Sun 11am–6pm.

④ Parkview Café. This family-friendly place is perfect for resting your feet and snacking on sandwiches, salads, and desserts. If you absolutely must check your e-mail, there's free Wi-Fi too. *Timken Center (old Casino Building), Dreyfous Dr.* ☎ 504/483-9476. *$.*

⑤ kids Carousel Gardens Amusement Park. Kids of all ages love to ride the "flying horses" on the antique wooden carousel. It was built in 1910 and is one of only 100 antique carousels left in the country. It and the 1906 pavilion are on the National Register of Historic Places. Other cool rides include bumper cars, a Red Baron miniplane, a Tilt-A-Whirl, a 40-foot (12m) fun slide, a Ferris wheel, and more. A miniature train takes riders on a 2½-mile (4km) trip through the park. ⏱ *45 min. Dreyfous Dr.* ☎ 504/483-9432. www.neworleanscitypark.com. *Admission $3 ages 3 and up, free 2 and under, rides $3 each, unlimited-ride band*

Kids make friends with a Storyland dragon.

\$17. Mid-Mar–Mid-Nov Fri–Sun 11am–6pm; extended hours June–Aug.

⑥ kids Storyland. More than 25 storybook-themed play areas feature colorful characters hand-sculpted by Mardi Gras float artists. Kids can climb in and out of Captain Hook's pirate ship, do a jig with the Three Little Pigs, explore the mouth of a whale with Pinocchio, or race up Jack & Jill's Hill. ⏱ *1 hr. Dreyfous Dr., next to Carousel Gardens.* ☎ 504/483-5402. *Admission $3, free 2 and under. Tues–Fri 11am–5pm, Sat–Sun 11am–6pm.*

⑦ City Park Tennis Center. One of the largest public tennis facilities in the South has hosted numerous tournaments over the years. *Wisner Tennis Center, near corner of Victory and Anseman aves., across from Storyland.* ☎ 504/483-9383. www.neworleanscitypark.com. *Hard courts $10 per hr., Rubico clay courts $13 per hr. Mon–Thurs 7am–10pm, Fri–Sun 7am–8pm.*

⑧ Roosevelt Mall. This shady half-mile (.8km) stretch of road and walkways is popular with joggers, dog walkers, and in-line skaters because it's one of the few New Orleans streets without significant bumps and potholes. You'll pass by kids playing softball in grassy fields and high school track-and-field teams sweating it out on the track. In 1937, President Franklin D. Roosevelt personally dedicated the mall and other WPA projects in the park, including nearby Tad Gormley Stadium. ⏱ *30 min. From Lelong Ave. to Marconi Dr.*

⑨ Tad Gormley Stadium. Built as part of the WPA efforts, the stadium has played host to a number of icons, including Roosevelt, Dorothy Lamour selling war bonds in

1942, entertainers Bob Hope in 1944 and Roy Rogers and Trigger in 1959, and the Beatles, who performed here in 1964. The stadium was remodeled in 1992 in preparation for the U.S. Olympic track-and-field trials that same year. ⏱ *10 min. Off Roosevelt Mall and Marconi Dr.*

⑩ **Suicide Oak.** Measuring more than 22 feet (6.6m) in circumference and 65 feet (20m) high with a 124-foot (37m) crown, Suicide Oak is one of the oldest and largest live oaks in the park. In the late 1800s and early 1900s many despondent people chose to end their lives here (thus the name), usually by hanging or self-inflicted gunshot wound. The last reported suicide took place in 1908. After the Huey P. Long Bridge was built in 1935, it replaced Suicide Oak's sordid purpose. Sadly, the tree has seen better centuries. It required repair twice in the 1980s when it lost a pair of humongous limbs. One of them remains on the ground and is estimated to be more than 150 years old. ⏱ *10 min. Corner of Marconi Dr. and Victory Ave.*

⑪ **Peristyle.** Built in 1907, this elegant neoclassical structure with massive Ionic columns originally served as a dance pavilion. Four concrete lions guard the structure, whose steps lead down to the bayou. There, you can watch the graceful swans and geese and ducks shamelessly beg for food from passersby. The Peristyle continues to set the scene for countless weddings, cocktail parties, picnics, and, of course, outdoor dances. ⏱ *15 min. Dreyfous Dr. overlooking Bayou Metairie.*

⑫ **Popp Bandstand.** Erected in 1917, the bandstand remains popular for outdoor concerts. U.S. Marine bandleader John Philip

Sousa performed here in 1928, and a live oak beside the bandstand was named in his honor. Unfortunately, the original Sousa Oak died in 1987. The Marines asked the Live Oak Society—of which all of the park's mature oaks are members in good standing—to name another oak for the famous American composer. The huge live oak to the left of the Peristyle is now known as the Sousa Oak. ⏱ *10 min. Dreyfous Dr. overlooking Bayou Metairie.*

⑬ **Fishing the Lagoons.** Unlike in Uptown's Audubon Park, fishing is allowed in City Park's 11 miles (18km) of lagoons. In their shallow depths, you'll (hopefully!) catch bass, catfish, and perch. Freshwater fishing permits are required by the State of Louisiana Department of Wildlife and Fisheries and are available for purchase online or by phone. *(www.wlf.louisiana.gov;* ☎ *888/765-2602).* ☎ *504/483-9371. www.neworleanscitypark.com. Resident fishing permit $9.50 (annual), $5 (1 day), plus service fee if ordered online/by phone. Open daily sunrise–sunset.*

⑭ **Couterie Forest Arboretum.** More than 280 bird species, from egrets to water thrushes, make for a birder's paradise. The 30-acre (12-hectare) park features fishing, birding, and hiking. ⏱ *½–1 hr. Harrison Ave. at Diagonal Dr. turnaround.* ☎ *504/482-4888. www.neworleanscitypark.com. Free admission. Open daily 8am–6pm.*

⑮ **Equest Farm.** This family-owned riding stable on 13 acres (5.2 hectares) offers horseback rides and English-riding lessons. You must call ahead for a reservation. ⏱ *1 hr. 1001 Filmore Ave.* ☎ *504/483-9398. www.equestfarm.com. Call for lesson or trail-ride fees. Tues–Sun 8am–7pm.*

Mississippi River

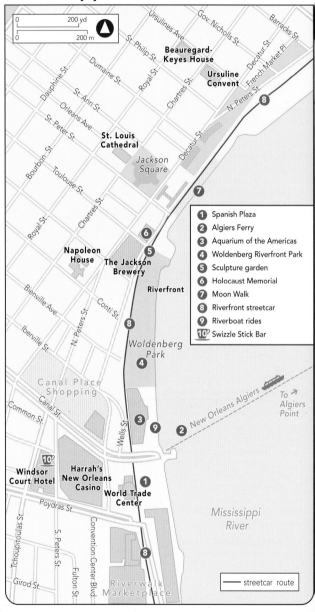

1 Spanish Plaza
2 Algiers Ferry
3 Aquarium of the Americas
4 Woldenberg Riverfront Park
5 Sculpture garden
6 Holocaust Memorial
7 Moon Walk
8 Riverfront streetcar
9 Riverboat rides
10 Swizzle Stick Bar

— streetcar route

New Orleans simply wouldn't exist without the Mississippi River. Early settlers recognized that the high ground tucked into a "crescent" of the river would make for a perfect international port, so the original Crescent City—the French Quarter—was founded in 1718. Today the riverfront remains a bustling public thoroughfare, offering sweeping views of the mythical waterway from land or ferry, with lush landscaping and evocative sculptures along the walking path as birds and street musicians fill the humid air with song. START: **Spanish Plaza, 1 Poydras Street.**

1 Spanish Plaza. Perhaps one of the most underrated romantic spots in the city, this beautifully tiled fountain with a view of the Mississippi was given to the city during the U.S. bicentennial in 1976 as a gift from Spain. Occasionally you'll see a couple get married here, then disappear back into the French Quarter. ⏲ *20 min. 1 Poydras St. at Mississippi River, beside Riverwalk Mall. Free admission. Daily 10am–6pm.*

2 Algiers Ferry. While not as old or architecturally pleasing as the other river ferry boats, this is the only one that's free and takes you across the river to Algiers Point, a historic neighborhood—bounded by Atlantic and Newton streets and the Mississippi—founded in 1719. ⏲ *5 min. Foot of Canal St. ☎ 504/376-8180 or 504/250-9109. www.friendsofthe ferry.org. Cars $1 (Algiers side only), pedestrians free. Mon–Thurs 7:15am–6:45pm, Fri 7:15am–8:15pm, Sat*

Views of the Mississippi and St. Louis Cathedral from the Algiers ferry.

10:45am–8:15pm, Sun 10:45am–6:15pm; leaves every 30 min.

3 kids Aquarium of the Americas. A shady bench at the sprawling entrance to the aquarium is a wonderful place to relax while the kids *ooh and aah* over the cute

Tiles line the Spanish Plaza fountain.

marine-life sculptures and real-life seagulls swooping in for crumbs. See p 47. ⏱ *20 min.–3 hr. (if you go inside). 1 Canal St.*

④ Woldenberg Riverfront Park. The park, just under 20 acres, is named after local philanthropist and civic leader Malcolm Woldenberg. ⏱ *30 min. Along river btw. aquarium and Jackson Square. Free admission.*

⑤ Sculpture garden. This informal sculpture garden has grown in size and artistic importance over the decades. My favorite piece is Robert Schoen's Carrara-marble figure *Old Man River*, a fitting tribute to the breadth and depth of the Mississippi. ⏱ *30 min. Inside Woldenberg Park. Free admission.*

⑥ Holocaust Memorial. Dedicated in 2003, this affecting memorial was rendered by Israeli sculptor Yaacov Agam. ⏱ *15–30 min. Inside Woldenberg Park. Free admission.*

⑦ kids Moon Walk. The riverside path offers a scenic view of the Mississippi River and the Crescent City Connection. See p 9. ⏱ *20 min. Across from Jackson Square along Mississippi River. Go before 8pm for safety's sake.*

⑧ Riverfront streetcar. Cherry-red vintage-looking streetcars run nearly 2 miles (3.2km) along the river, past old wharves and warehouses behind the French Market, giving you a glimpse of the glory days of river-run industry. ⏱ *20 min. Thalia St. to Esplanade Ave. ☎ 504/248-3900. www.norta.com. Fare $1.50 one-way.*

⑨ kids Riverboat rides. Enjoy the city skyline from the steamboat *Natchez*, one of only six steam-powered stern-wheelers on the Mississippi; or the New Orleans Paddlewheels Company's *Creole Queen*. Food and special dinner tours are available; save your money and dine elsewhere. ⏱ *2 hr. Docked near the aquarium and the end of Canal St. Steamboat Natchez: ☎ 800/365-2628 or 504/586-8777. www.steamboatnatchez.com. Admission $43 adults, $21.50 children 6–12. Dinner included $72.50 adults, $34 children 6–12, $14 children 2–5. New Orleans Paddlewheels Company: ☎ 800/445-4109 or 504/529-4567. www.neworleanspaddlewheels.com. Admission $40 adults, $20 children 6–12. Dinner included $69 adults, $34 children 6–12, $10 children 3–5. Call for cruise days/times.*

⑩ Swizzle Stick Bar. Stop in for a swanky end-of-tour cocktail at this hip and classy bar inside the Loews New Orleans Hotel. *300 Poydras St., ☎ 504/595-3305. $. ●*

The Creole Queen.

Dining Best Bets

Best **Celebrity-Chef Meal**
★★ Emeril's $$$
800 Tchoupitoulas St. (p 104)

Best **Creole Restaurant**
★★ Arnaud's $$$ *813 Bienville St.*
(p 101)

Best **Diner**
★ Mother's $ *401 Poydras St.*
(p 106)

Best **Burger**
★ Port of Call $ *838 Esplanade Ave.*
(p 107)

Best **Fried Chicken**
★ Willie Mae's Scotch House $
2401 St. Ann St. (p 108)

Best **Bakery**
★★ Croissant d'Or $ *617 Ursulines*
Ave. (p 103)

Best **Creole/Acadian**
Restaurant
★★★ Brigtsen's $$ *723 Dante St.*
(p 102)

Most **Worth the Wait**
★★ Irene's Cuisine $
539 St. Philip St. (p 105)

Most **Romantic**
★★★ Upperline $$
1413 Upperline St. (p 108)

Best **Breakfast**
★★★ Elizabeth's $$ *601 Gallier St.*
(p 104)

Best **Neighborhood Italian**
★★ Liuzza's $ *3636 Bienville St.*
(p 106)

Best **Po' Boy**
★★ Guy's $ *5259 Magazine St.*
(p 105)

Best **Place to Find Locals**
★ Riccobono's Panola Street Café
$, *7801 Panola St. (p 107)*

Best **New Southern**
★★★ Dick & Jenny's $$
4501 Tchoupitoulas St. (p 103)

Best **Jazz Brunch**
★★ Palace Café $$, *605 Canal St.*
(p 106)

Best **Four-Star Meal at**
Two-Star Prices
★★ Ciro's Cote Sud $$
7918 Maple St. (p 102)

Best **Ice Cream**
★★★ The Creole Creamery $
4924 Prytania St. (p 103)

Best **Burrito**
★★ Taqueria Corona $
5932 Magazine St. (p 108)

Best **Meal in a Truck Bed**
★★★ Jacques-Imo's $$
8324 Oak St. (p 105)

Previous page: Crawfish are a New Orleans tradition.

French Quarter Dining

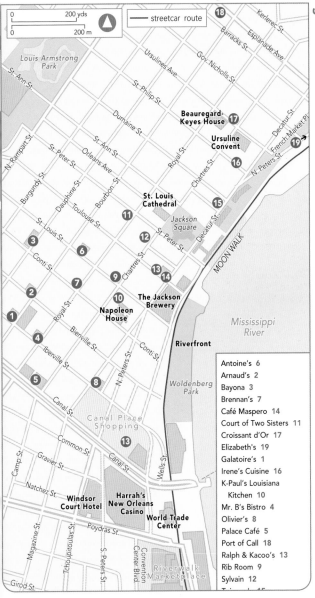

Antoine's 6
Arnaud's 2
Bayona 3
Brennan's 7
Café Maspero 14
Court of Two Sisters 11
Croissant d'Or 17
Elizabeth's 19
Galatoire's 1
Irene's Cuisine 16
K-Paul's Louisiana
    Kitchen 10
Mr. B's Bistro 4
Olivier's 8
Palace Café 5
Port of Call 18
Ralph & Kacoo's 13
Rib Room 9
Sylvain 12

Central Business District Dining

Emeril's 5
Herbsaint 1
Mother's 2
The Grill Room 4
Restaurant August 3

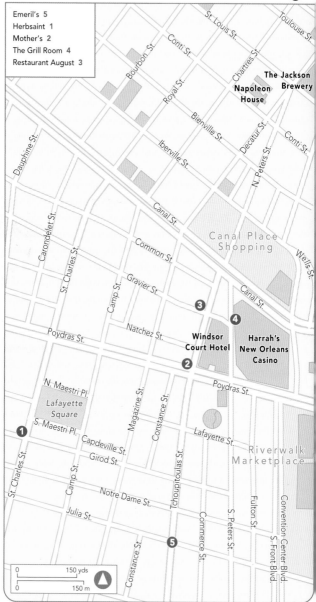

Uptown Dining

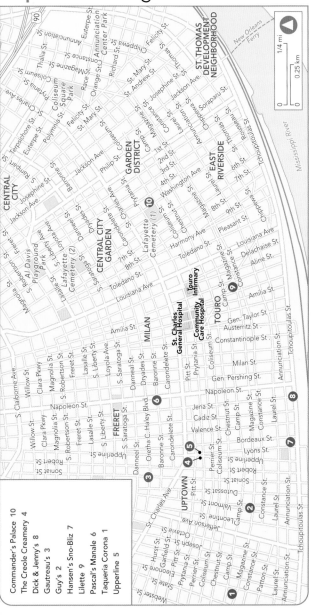

Commander's Palace 10
The Creole Creamery 4
Dick & Jenny's 8
Gautreau's 3
Guy's 2
Hansen's Sno-Bliz 7
Lilette 9
Pascal's Manale 6
Taqueria Corona 1
Upperline 5

Carrollton/Mid-City Dining

Brigtsen's 2
Ciro's Cote Sud 1
Dooky Chase 8
Jacques-Imo's Café 3
Liuzza's 6
Ralph's on the Park 5
Riccobono's Panola Street Café 4
Willie Mae's Scotch House 7

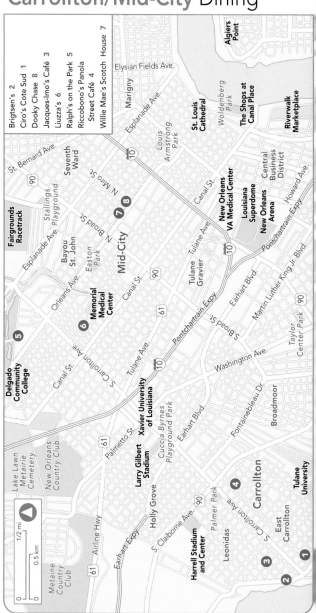

Dining A to Z

★ **Antoine's** FRENCH QUARTER
FRENCH/CREOLE A truly original
mom 'n' pop restaurant, Antoine's
has evolved into one of New
Orleans's most lauded and popular
upscale establishments under the
guidance of the same family for
more than 160 years. Start with oysters Rockefeller and finish with the
flashy baked Alaska; you can't go
wrong with anything in between.
713 St. Louis St. ☎ *504/581-4422.
www.antoines.com. Reservations recommended. No sandals or T-shirts;
collared shirts for men. Entrees $34–
$40. AE, DC, MC, V. Lunch & dinner
Mon–Sat, brunch Sun. Map p 97.*

Antoine's famous baked Alaska.

recommended. Business casual.
*Entrees $19–$38. AE, DC, DISC, MC,
V. Dinner nightly, jazz brunch Sun.
Map p 97.*

★★ **Arnaud's** FRENCH QUARTER
CREOLE Old New Orleans culture
haunts you like a specter here, from
the moody antique lighting to the
dark, butter-rich sauces on every
plate. Expect traditional crab cakes
and shrimp Creole as well as fantastic fish dishes and top-notch steaks.
Dare to venture up the creaky stairs
for a peek at founder Germaine
Wells's early-20th-century haute
Carnival couture. *813 Bienville St.*
☎ *504/523-5433. www.arnauds
restaurant.com. Reservations*

★★★ **Bayona** FRENCH QUARTER
INTERNATIONAL Chef-owner
Susan Spicer tempts the bravest of
palates in a romantic 200-year-old
Creole cottage setting. She prepares local sense-surprising seafood riches like crawfish, shrimp,
and redfish with an international
flair. Bayona's name reflects the
original Spanish name for Dauphine
Street, *Camino de Bayona.
430 Dauphine St.* ☎ *504/525-4455.*

*Upstairs at Arnaud's is a collection of Mardi Gras costumes worn by the restaurant's
founder.*

www.bayona.com. *Reservations required for dinner. Entrees $28–$38. AE, DC, DISC, MC, V. Lunch Wed– Sat, dinner Mon–Sat. Map p 97.*

Brennan's FRENCH QUARTER *CREOLE/FRENCH* Breakfast at Brennan's is indulgent and satisfying, although your $50 will go farther (and you'll have more breathing room) if you come for lunch or dinner instead. **NOTE:** At the time of this writing, the restaurant had temporarily closed due to Brennan family drama. New owners—which include Ralph Brennan—promise something in the works. *417 Royal St.* ☎ *504/525-9711. www.brennans neworleans.com. Reservations recommended. Map p 97.*

★★★ **Brigtsen's** CARROLLTON *CREOLE/ACADIAN* The moment you step inside this tucked away 19th-century Victorian cottage, hostess Marna Brigtsen will make you feel at home. Chef Frank Brigtsen insists on fresh seasonal ingredients, produced locally whenever possible; your taste buds can tell the difference. When in season, order the seafood platter, piled high with drum, shrimp, crawfish, oysters, and scallops. *723 Dante St.* ☎ *504/861-7610. www.brigtsens. com. Reservations required. Entrees $24–$35. AE, DC, MC, V. Dinner Tues–Sat. Map p 100.*

Kids Café Maspero FRENCH QUARTER *SANDWICHES/ SEAFOOD* Perhaps the only sandwich place I know that doesn't serve po' boys, but the familiar finger food is fun for little ones. *601 Decatur St.* ☎ *504/523-6250. Entrees $4–$9. Lunch & dinner daily. Map p 97.*

★★ **Ciro's Cote Sud** CARROLLTON *FRENCH/PIZZA* When a French chef buys an Italian pizza parlor you get sinfully rich Provençal fare and thin-crust pizza on the same menu. Skip the 'za and go for

Chef Frank Brigtsen.

the shrimp, Louisiana crawfish tails, and scallops in a creamy curry sauce. Spicy and smooth all in one forkful. *7918 Maple St.* ☎ *504/866-9551. www.cotesudrestaurant.com. Entrees $13–$22. No credit cards. Dinner nightly. Map p 100.*

★★★ **Commander's Palace** GARDEN DISTRICT *CREOLE* The Brennan family is known for spotting talent—legendary chefs Paul Prudhomme, Emeril Lagasse, and Jamie Shannon all got their start here—so it's no surprise that executive chef Tory McPhail won the James Beard Foundation's Best Chef: South award

There's a flavor for everyone at the Creole Creamery.

in 2013. The first time I ever experienced soft-shell crab was here, and it remains the most tender, flavorful seafood I've ever tasted. *1403 Washington Ave.* ☎ *504/899-8221. www.commanderspalace.com. Upscale dress, jackets preferred at dinner; no shorts or T-shirts. Entrees $36–$45, brunch $27–$32. Lunch Mon–Fri, dinner nightly, jazz brunch Sat–Sun. Map p 99.*

kids Court of Two Sisters
FRENCH QUARTER *CREOLE*
The exposed brick, soothing fountain, and jazz music add up to a stronger impression than the food, which includes takes on Creole-style fish, fowl, and beef. Reasonably priced children's menu available. *613 Royal St.* ☎ *504/522-7261. www.courtoftwosisters.com. Reservations recommended. Entrees $25–$35, brunch $29. AE, DC, DISC, MC, V. Brunch & dinner daily. Map p 97.*

★★★ kids The Creole Creamery
UPTOWN/LAKEVIEW *DESSERT*
This neighborhood ice cream parlor looks like a throwback to the 1950s but boasts totally modern taste combinations. Have you ever tried flavors like lavender honey, red velvet cake, or Mexican hot chocolate? If you can't decide, choose an ice cream sampler with four or six mini-scoops. *4924 Prytania St.* ☎ *504/894-8680 and 6260 Vicksburg St* ☎ *504/482-2924. www.creolecreamery.com. Everything under $10. No credit cards. Uptown hours: Sun–Thurs noon–10pm, Fri–Sat noon–11pm. Lakeview hours: Sun–Thurs 2–9pm, Fri–Sat 2–10pm. Map p 99.*

★★ Croissant d'Or
FRENCH QUARTER *SANDWICHES/PASTRIES*
For years we met friends every Sunday at this quiet French bakery to

The sign outside the Croissant d'Or.

sip delicious iced coffee and munch flaky chocolate croissants, mini apple tarts, quiche, and crunchy tuna-salad sandwiches. *617 Ursulines Ave.* ☎ *504/524-4663. www.croissantdornola.com. Entrees $8 and under. MC, V. Wed–Mon 6:30am–3pm. Map p 97.*

★★★ Dick & Jenny's
UPTOWN *CREOLE*
The slow-food revolution meets youthful vitality. Dishes such as ginger-crusted salmon and stuffed pork tenderloin are absolutely worth the wait. *4501 Tchoupitoulas St.* ☎ *504/894-9880. www.dickandjennys.com. Reservations for parties of 5 or more. Entrees $16–$28. AE, DISC, MC, V. Lunch Tues–Fri, dinner Mon–Sat. Map p 99.*

Dooky Chase
TREME *CREOLE/SOUL FOOD*
Upscale soul food from nonagenarian chef-matriarch Leah Chase and grandson Edgar "Dooky" Chase IV, a Le Cordon Bleu

Soft-shell crab at Dick & Jenny's.

grad. *2301 Orleans Ave.* ☎ *504/821-0600. www.dookychaserestaurant.com. Entrees $9–$20. No credit cards. Lunch Tues–Fri dine in or take out, dinner Fri. Map p 100.*

★★★ **Elizabeth's** BYWATER *BREAKFAST/CREOLE* Yeah, it's out of the way, but I'd drive hundreds of miles for its sweet, crispy praline bacon. *601 Gallier St.* ☎ *504/944-9272. www.elizabeths restaurantnola.com. Entrees $9—$17. MC, V. Breakfast & lunch daily, dinner Mon–Sat. Map p 97.*

★★ **Emeril's** CENTRAL BUSINESS DISTRICT *CREOLE/NEW AMERICAN* Who doesn't know the "Bam" man? His star has fallen a bit from overexposure, but when he's in the kitchen, the food and service are all kicked up a notch. *800 Tchoupitoulas St.* ☎ *504/528-9393. www.emerilsrestaurants.com/ emerils-new-orleans. Reservations recommended. Entrees $25–$45; degustation menu available (arranged in advance). AE, DC, DISC, MC, V. Lunch Mon–Fri, dinner nightly. Map p 98.*

★★ **Galatoire's** FRENCH QUARTER *FRENCH* Grab Tennessee Williams's table (in the main window, in front of the word "Restaurant") and prepare to be satiated by extravagant multicourse French meals prepared from recipes that have been in the family since 1905. *209 Bourbon St.* ☎ *504/525-2021. www.galatoires.com. Reservations accepted for 2nd-floor dining room only. Jackets required for dinner and on Sun. Entrees $19–$34. AE, DC, DISC, MC, V. Lunch & dinner Tues–Sun. Map p 97.*

★★ **Gautreau's** UPTOWN *FRENCH* The flickering candlelight, Parisian-style *trompe l'oeil* on the walls, and tin ceiling set a romantic mood in this brilliantly converted neighborhood drugstore. (You can still see the original antique apothecary cases, which now display wine and liquor.) The menu changes every 6 weeks to take advantage of seasonal seafood and produce. *1728 Soniat St.* ☎ *504/899-7397. www.gautreaus restaurant.com. Reservations recommended. Entrees $25–$35. AE, MC, V. Dinner Mon–Sat. Map p 99.*

★★ **The Grill Room** CENTRAL BUSINESS DISTRICT *INTERNATIONAL* Indulge without being excessive. Delights include lump crab cakes, Colorado lamb chops,

Elizabeth's praline bacon.

Preparing the po'boys at Guy's.

and seared diver scallops. *300 Gravier St.* ☎ *504/522-1994. www.grill roomneworleans.com. Reservations recommended. Entrees $24–$38. AE, DC, DISC, MC, V. Breakfast, lunch & dinner daily, jazz brunch Sun. Map p 98.*

★★ **Guy's** UPTOWN *SAND-WICHES* Owner Marvin Matherne will personally make you the best grilled-shrimp po' boy you've ever had. Be sure to grab lots of napkins because that fresh French bread can only soak up so much buttery juice. *5259 Magazine St.* ☎ *504/891-5025. Sandwiches $6.50–$12. No credit cards. Lunch Mon–Sat. Map p 99.*

★★ **Hansen's Sno-Bliz** UPTOWN *DESSERT* Ernest and Mary Hansen founded this family favorite back in 1939; their granddaughter Ashley continues to run it today. Ernest's snowball machine invention creates such finely shaved ice that it's like eating snowflakes. While waiting in line, check out the fun wall of photos of past patrons. *4801 Tchoupitoulas St.* ☎ *504/891-9788. www. snobliz.com. Cash only. Tues–Sun 1–7pm, open spring–fall. Map p 99.*

★ **Herbsaint** CENTRAL BUSINESS DISTRICT *FRENCH/NEW AMERICAN* Chef-owner Donald Link offers hearty Southern comfort food such as pork belly, gumbo, okra, and collard greens in a casual bistro setting. *701 St. Charles Ave.* ☎ *504/524-4114. www.herbsaint. com. Reservations recommended. Entrees $26–$34. AE, DC, DISC, MC, V. Lunch Mon–Fri, dinner Mon–Sat. Map p 98.*

★★ **Irene's Cuisine** FRENCH QUARTER *FRENCH/ITALIAN* Good things come to those who wait, namely a fine Italian meal, mood-altering desserts, and brisk service. Despite plenty of competition, shellfish lovers claim its charbroiled oysters topped with melted cheese and bits of bacon are the best in the city. *539 St. Philip St.* ☎ *504/529-8811. Limited reservations if space available. Entrees $18–$38. AE, MC, V. Dinner Mon–Sat. Map p 97.*

★★★ **Jacques-Imo's Café** CARROLLTON *CREOLE/SOUL FOOD* Enjoy your stuffed pork chop or fried chicken seated in the truck parked outside and be the envy of all. *8324 Oak St.* ☎ *504/861-0886. www.jacques-imos.com. Reservations required for parties of 5 or more. Entrees $19–$37. AE, DC, DISC, MC, V. Dinner Mon–Sat. Map p 100.*

★★ K-Paul's Louisiana Kitchen FRENCH QUARTER

CAJUN Chef-owner Paul Prud-homme's signature blackened red-fish remains a favorite even if it's gone mainstream. You'll eat well but pay way too much. *416 Chartres St.* ☎ *504/596-2530. www.kpauls. com. Reservations recommended. Business casual. Entrees $27–$36. AE, DC, DISC, MC, V. Lunch Thurs–Sat, dinner Mon–Sat. Map p 97.*

★ Lilette UPTOWN CREOLE/ FRENCH

Classic French fare meets experimental Creole flair in a cozy corner bistro. *3637 Magazine St.* ☎ *504/895-1636. www.lilette restaurant.com. Reservations recommended. Entrees $22–$37. AE, DISC, MC, V. Lunch & dinner Tues–Sat. Map p 99.*

★★ kids Liuzza's MID-CITY ITALIAN/SANDWICHES/SEAFOOD

Locals have loved the simple comfort food here—including pastas, salads, and sandwiches—since 1947. Massive frosty mugs of Abita beer are a must. *3636 Bienville St.* ☎ *504/482-9120. www.liuzzas.com. Entrees $10–$20. No credit cards. Lunch daily, dinner Tues–Sat. Map p 100.*

★ kids Mother's CENTRAL BUSINESS DISTRICT BREAKFAST/ CREOLE/SANDWICHES/SHORT

ORDER Nothing fancy, just really good, greasy diner food. *401 Poy-dras St.* ☎ *504/523-9656. www. mothersrestaurant.net. Entrees $9–$25. AE, DISC, MC, V. Breakfast, lunch & dinner daily. Map p 98.*

Mr. B's Bistro FRENCH QUARTER CONTEMPORARY CREOLE

A Brennan family favorite among businesspeople and politicians brokering lunchtime deals. The crab cakes and Gumbo Ya-Ya are excellent. *201 Royal St.* ☎ *504/523-2078. www.mrbsbistro.com. Entrees $26–$38. AE, DC, DISC, MC, V. Lunch & dinner Mon–Sat, jazz brunch Sun. Map p 97.*

★ Olivier's FRENCH QUARTER CREOLE/FRENCH

Old-fashioned family cooking is in chef Armand Olivier's blood. Some of his recipes—such as Creole rabbit and crawfish étouffée—have been passed down through generations. *204 Decatur St.* ☎ *504/525-7734. www.olivierscreole.com. Reservations recommended. Entrees $18–$26. AE, DC, DISC, MC, V. Lunch Tues–Sat, dinner nightly. Map p 97.*

★★ Palace Café FRENCH QUARTER CONTEMPORARY CREOLE

Part of the Brennan family of restaurants, Palace Café offers creative takes on seafood, pork, and seasonal specialties. And for dessert? I

Dinner in the truck at Jacques-Imo's.

Onion rings and a cold one at Liuzza's.

have four words for you: white chocolate bread pudding. You're welcome. *605 Canal St. ☎ 504/523-1661. www.palacecafe.com. Reservations recommended. Entrees $23–$34. AE, DC, DISC, MC, V. Lunch & dinner daily, brunch Sun. Map p 97.*

Pascal's Manale UPTOWN *ITALIAN/SEAFOOD/STEAKHOUSE* Skip the steak and go for the barbecued shrimp and raw oysters. *1838 Napoleon Ave. ☎ 504/895-4877. Reservations recommended. Entrees $17–$34. AE, DC, DISC, MC, V. Lunch Mon–Fri, dinner Mon–Sat. Map p 99.*

★ Port of Call FRENCH QUARTER *HAMBURGERS/SANDWICHES* If you're going to eat a burger in New Orleans, this is the place to get it. *838 Esplanade Ave. ☎ 504/523-0120. www.portofcallnola.com. Entrees $10–$26. AE, MC, V. Lunch & dinner daily. Map p 97.*

kids Ralph & Kacoo's FRENCH QUARTER *CREOLE/SEAFOOD* Huge portions and decent prices make this chain—serving fried crawfish, onion rings, oysters, and the like—better than some. *519 Toulouse St. ☎ 504/522-5226. www. ralphandkacoos.com. Reservations recommended. Entrees $16–$33. AE,*

DC, DISC, MC, V. Lunch Fri–Sun, dinner nightly. Map p 97.

★ Ralph's on the Park MID-CITY *CREOLE/SEAFOOD* This restaurant in a historic neighborhood features a lovely view of City Park's giant oaks. Oh, and the food—which includes braised lamb, crawfish salad, and baked oysters Ralph—is good too. *900 City Park Ave. ☎ 504/488-1000. www.ralphsonthepark.com. Reservations recommended. Entrees $23–$46. AE, MC, V. Lunch Wed–Fri, dinner nightly, brunch Sun. Map p 100.*

★★★ Restaurant August CENTRAL BUSINESS DISTRICT *CONTEMPORARY FRENCH* Executive chef John Besh applies his native Louisiana instincts to signature French dishes. *301 Tchoupitoulas St. ☎ 504/299-9777. www. restaurantaugust.com. Reservations recommended. Entrees $22–$40. AE, DC, MC, V. Lunch Mon–Fri, dinner nightly. Map p 98.*

Rib Room FRENCH QUARTER *SEAFOOD/STEAKHOUSE* Sometimes you just need the simple perfection of prime rib. *621 St. Louis St. ☎ 504/529-7046. www.ribroomneworleans.com. Reservations recommended. Business casual. Entrees $24–$38. AE, DC, DISC, MC, V. Breakfast, lunch & dinner daily, brunch Sun. Map p 97.*

★ kids Riccobono's Panola Street Café CARROLLTON *BREAKFAST/SANDWICHES* Welcome to a true neighborhood hangout, where locals gather with family and friends to catch up over free coffee refills, eggs made any way you like 'em, and the usual breakfast staples of sausage, bacon, and biscuits. (Breakfast served all day.) The college-student servers give you quick, attentive service. *7801 Panola St. ☎ 504/314-1810. Entrees $7–$20. AE, MC,*

Upperline restaurant.

V. Breakfast & lunch daily. Map p 100.

★★ Sylvain FRENCH QUARTER *BISTRO* Named for the first opera performed in the U.S., which was staged in New Orleans in 1796, Sylvain entertains all of your senses. The thoughtfully renovated three-story carriage house it's set in once belonged to an infamous Storyville madam. The braised beef cheeks are a must, and dessert can only be the chocolate pot de crème. *625 Chartres St.* ☎ *504/265-8123. www.sylvainnola.com. Entrees $16–$24. AE, DC, DISC, MC, V. Lunch Fri–Sun, dinner nightly. Map p 97.*

★★ kids Taqueria Corona UPTOWN *MEXICAN* Coeds, Uptown families, suburbanites, and tourists all come here for the cheap, plentiful, outstanding food. Start with crispy hot chips, tangy pico de gallo, and a margarita. For a taste of everything at a ridiculously good price, choose one of the combination platters. *5932 Magazine St.* ☎ *504/897-3974. www.taqueriacorona.com. Entrees $8–$15. AE, MC, V. Lunch & dinner daily. Map p 99.*

★ Tujague's FRENCH QUARTER *CREOLE* Old-fashioned and set in its ways; what do you expect from a restaurant dating back to 1856? Beef brisket and shrimp rémoulade are typical offerings. *823 Decatur St.* ☎ *504/525-8676. www.tujagues.com. Reservations recommended. 6 courses $36–$45. AE, DC, DISC, MC, V. Sat–Sun lunch, dinner nightly. Map p 97.*

★★★ Upperline UPTOWN *CREOLE/ECLECTIC* Owner-hostess JoAnn Clevenger makes a point of visiting every table to chat with diners, so do your best to tear yourself away from those fried green tomatoes topped with tangy shrimp rémoulade. *1413 Upperline St.* ☎ *504/891-9822. www.upperline.com. Reservations recommended. Entrees $20–$30; 3 courses prix fixe $40. AE, DC, MC, V. Dinner Wed–Sun. Map p 97.*

★ Willie Mae's Scotch House MID-CITY *SOUL FOOD* Sink your teeth into the juicy fried chicken served with a side of creamy butter beans. *2401 St. Ann St.* ☎ *504/822-9503. Everything under $15. AE, DISC, MC. Lunch daily. Map p 100.* ●

Nightlife Best Bets

Best **Burlesque**
★ One Eyed Jacks, *615 Toulouse St. (p 119)*

Best **Happy Hour**
★★ Bar Tonique, *820 N. Rampart St. (p 115)*

Best **Dive Bar**
★ Snake & Jake's Xmas Club Lounge, *7612 Oak St. (p 117)*

Best **Late-Late Spot**
★ The Dungeon, *738 Toulouse St. (p 119)*

Best **Gay & Lesbian**
★★★ Oz, *800 Bourbon St. (p 119)*

Best **Downtown Bar**
★★ Ampersand, *1100 Tulane Ave. (p 119)*

Best **Cajun Dancing**
★ Mulate's, *201 Julia St. (p 118)*

Best **Historic Bar**
★★★ Napoleon House, *500 Chartres St. (p 120)*

Best **Karaoke**
★ Cat's Meow, *701 Bourbon St. (p 121)*

Best **Jazz Club**
★★ Snug Harbor, *626 Frenchmen St. (p 120)*

Best **Jukebox**
★ F&M Patio Bar, *4841 Tchoupitoulas St. (p 119)*

Previous page: A bartender at Molly's at the Market pours a local favorite, Abita Springs beer.
Below: Irvin Mayfield performs at Snug Harbor.

French Quarter Nightlife

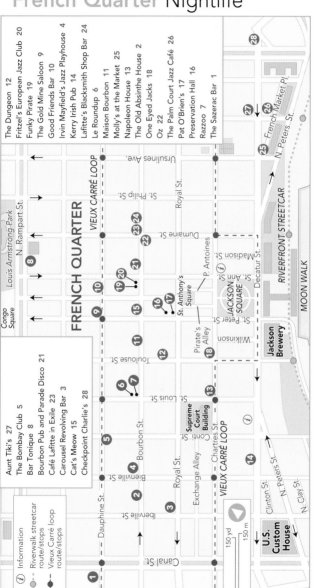

The Dungeon 12
Fritzel's European Jazz Club 20
Funky Pirate 19
The Gold Mine Saloon 9
Good Friends Bar 10
Irvin Mayfield's Jazz Playhouse 4
Kerry Irish Pub 14
Lafitte's Blacksmith Shop Bar 24
Le Roundup 6
Maison Bourbon 11
Molly's at the Market 25
Napoleon House 13
The Old Absinthe House 2
One Eyed Jacks 18
Oz 22
The Palm Court Jazz Café 26
Pat O'Brien's 17
Preservation Hall 16
Razzoo 7
The Sazerac Bar 1

Aunt Tiki's 27
The Bombay Club 5
Bar Tonique 8
Bourbon Pub and Parade Disco 21
Café Lafitte in Exile 23
Carousel Revolving Bar 3
Cat's Meow 15
Checkpoint Charlie's 28

(i) Information
Riverwalk streetcar route/stops
Vieux Carré loop route/stops

Louis Armstrong Park
Congo Square
N. Rampart St.

FRENCH QUARTER
VIEUX CARRÉ LOOP

Ursulines Ave.
St. Philip St.
Royal St.
Dumaine St.
St. Anthony's Square
P. Antoines
St. Ann St.
JACKSON SQUARE
St. Peter St.
Pirate's Alley
Wilkinson
Madison St.
Decatur St.
Jackson Brewery

RIVERFRONT STREETCAR
MOON WALK
French Market Pl.
N. Peters St.

Toulouse St.
St. Louis St.
Supreme Court Building
Conti St.
Exchange Alley
Chartres St.
VIEUX CARRÉ LOOP

Dauphine St.
Bourbon St.
Bienville St.
Royal St.
Iberville St.

Canal St.

Clinton St.
N. Peters St.
N. Clay St.

U.S. Custom House

150 yd
150 m

Uptown Nightlife

F&M Patio Bar 4
Le Bon Temps Roulé 3
St. Joe's Bar 2
Snake & Jake's Xmas Club Lounge 1
Tipitina's 5

Central Business District Nightlife

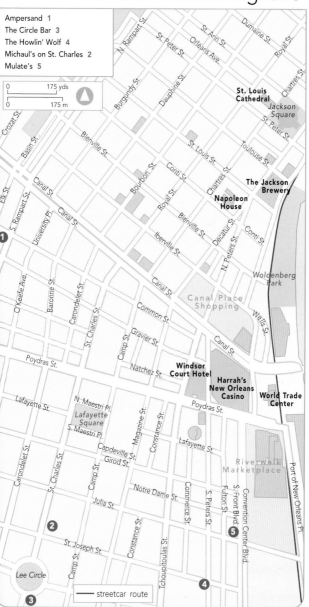

Ampersand 1
The Circle Bar 3
The Howlin' Wolf 4
Michaul's on St. Charles 2
Mulate's 5

| 0 | 175 yds |
| 0 | 175 m |

St. Louis Cathedral

Jackson Square

The Jackson Brewery

Napoleon House

Woldenberg Park

Canal Place Shopping

Windsor Court Hotel

Harrah's New Orleans Casino

World Trade Center

Lafayette Square

Riverwalk Marketplace

Lee Circle

— streetcar route

Faubourg Marigny/Bywater
Nightlife

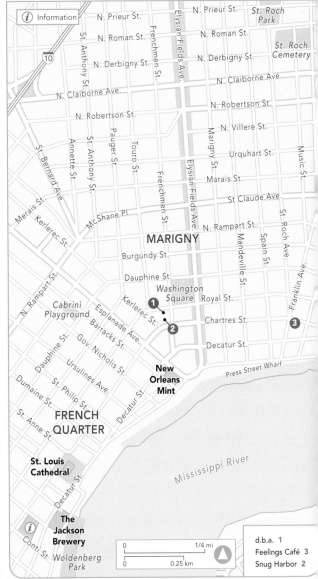

Information

N. Prieur St.
N. Prieur St.
St. Roch Park
N. Roman St.
N. Roman St.
St. Roch Cemetery
N. Derbigny St.
N. Derbigny St.
N. Claiborne Ave.
N. Claiborne Ave.
N. Robertson St.
N. Robertson St.
N. Villere St.
St. Anthony St.
Annette St.
St. Anthony St.
Pauger St.
Touro St.
Frenchmen St.
Elysian Fields Ave.
Marigny St.
Urquhart St.
Marais St.
St Claude Ave.
St. Bernard Ave.
Merais St.
Kerlerec St.
McShane Pl.
Music St.
St. Roch Ave.
N. Rampart St.
Spain St.
Mandeville St.
Franklin Ave.

MARIGNY

Burgundy St.
Dauphine St.
Washington Square
Royal St.
N. Rampart St.
Cabrini Playground
Esplanade Ave.
Kerlerec St.
Barracks St.
Gov. Nicholis St.
Ursulines Ave.
St. Philip St.
Decatur St.
Chartres St.
Decatur St.
Press Street Wharf
Dauphine St.
Dumaine St.
St. Anne St.

New Orleans Mint

FRENCH QUARTER

St. Louis Cathedral

Decatur St.

The Jackson Brewery

Conti St.
Woldenberg Park

Mississippi River

0   1/4 mi
0   0.25 km

d.b.a. **1**
Feelings Café **3**
Snug Harbor **2**

Carrollton/Mid-City Nightlife

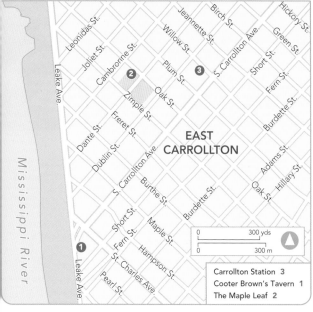

Mississippi River

Carrollton Station **3**
Cooter Brown's Tavern **1**
The Maple Leaf **2**

0   300 yds
0   300 m

EAST CARROLLTON

Nightlife A to Z

Bars

Aunt Tiki's FRENCH QUARTER
Like the name suggests, this is a
good place to blend in with an eclectic crowd. And the no-frills decor
means you won't be gouged for
drinks like at some Quarter establishments. *1207 Decatur St.* ☎ *504/
680-8454. No cover. Map p 111.*

★★ Bar Tonique FRENCH
QUARTER Classic or creative cocktails without pretense amid a good
mix of neighborhood locals. As candles flicker against exposed brick,
sip a Blanche DuBois and travel back
in time. *820 N. Rampart St.* ☎ *504/
324-6045. No cover. Map p 111.*

Le Bon Temps Roulé UPTOWN
Be prepared for a party crowd of

coeds and neighborhood regulars
who know how to pass a good time
drinking Abita with greasy burgers

*Aunt Tiki's, a comfortable, no-frills bar in
the French Quarter.*

Patrons at Bar Tonique.

and jamming to popular local acts on the weekends. *4801 Magazine St.* ☎ *504/897-3448 or 504/895-8117. No cover. Map p 112.*

★★★ The Maple Leaf

CARROLLTON   Though small, the patio out back gives you a little breathing room and dancing space, which you'll definitely need if regular favorite Rebirth Brass Band is playing. College kids can run amok, but you'll find their profs here too, more often than not. *8316 Oak St.* ☎ *504/866-9359. Cover $5–$15. Map p 115.*

★ Molly's at the Market

FRENCH QUARTER   You'll get the local scoop any night of the week thanks to a bizarre though typically New Orleans blend of patrons who always have a story to tell. *1107 Decatur St.* ☎ *504/525-5169. No cover. Map p 111.*

★★ St. Joe's Bar UPTOWN

After a day of shopping on Magazine Street, relax at the dark, narrow bar or head back to a seat on the tropical patio; either way, you'll get attentive service and a little room to kick back—unless it's super late on the weekend and overrun

The crowd dances to Rebirth Brass Band at the Maple Leaf.

by college kids and single 20-somethings. *5535 Magazine St.* ☎ *504/899-3744. No cover. Map p 112.*

★ **Snake & Jake's Xmas Club Lounge** CARROLLTON Only venture here if you like Christmas decorations year-round, dogs hanging out at their masters' feet, soul and R & B pumping from the jukebox, and really, really dark corners. *7612 Oak St.* ☎ *504/861-2802. www.snakeandjakes.com. No cover. Map p 112.*

★★★ **Tipitina's** UPTOWN I will never, ever forgive my college roommate for going to a show here without me and spotting Bono in the audience. No matter what musical genre gets you off your feet—folk, rock, country, R & B— you'll find it here and, occasionally, a famous face in the crowd. I prefer the balcony for people-watching and dancing because there's more room to groove. Learn to eat and dance like a Cajun at the "Fais Do-do" every Sunday afternoon. *501 Napoleon Ave.* ☎ *504/895-8477 or* ☎ *504/897-3943. www.tipitinas. com. Cover $5–$15. Map p 112.*

Blues Bars

Funky Pirate FRENCH QUARTER Passionate blues lovers flock here for Chicago-style musings, often belted out by blues king Big Al Carson, who plays here most nights to a good-size but not rambunctious crowd. *727 Bourbon St.* ☎ *504/523-1960. http://thefunkypirate.com. No cover. One-drink minimum. Map p 111.*

Cajun/Zydeco Venues

kids **Michaul's on St. Charles** CENTRAL BUSINESS DISTRICT

Funky Pirate.

On the downside, Michaul's caters more to conventioneers and the decor has a banquet hall feel. But on the plus side, enjoy free Cajun dance lessons, live music, and boatloads of spicy crawfish. *840 St. Charles Ave.* ☎ *800/563-4055 or 504/522-5517. www.michauls.com. No cover. Map p 113.*

★★★ **Mid-City Lanes Rock 'n' Bowl** MID-CITY You can't be a guest at my house and not come here to experience one of New Orleans's more bizarre offerings— bowling and dancing to live Cajun and zydeco music. *3000 S. Carrollton Ave.* ☎ *504/861-1700. www. rockandbowl.com. Shoe rental $1. Lane rental $24/hr. Map p 2.*

Tipitina's.

The bowling lanes at Mid-City Lanes Rock 'n' Bowl.

★ **Mulate's** CENTRAL BUSINESS DISTRICT   Owner Kerry Boutté—born in the small Cajun town of Arnaudville—opened this popular joint nearly 30 years ago to bring live Cajun music, dancing, and food to the masses. It's the next best thing if you can't travel to Lafayette to experience the real deal. *201 Julia St.* ☎ *504/522-1492. www. mulates.com. No cover. Map p 113.*

Dance Clubs

Gold Mine Saloon FRENCH QUARTER   Under-30 hipsters work up a sweat to techno and whatever's popular, usually followed by a sweet flaming Dr. Pepper shot for extra energy. Poetry readings are held Thursday nights. *701 Dauphine St.* ☎ *504/586-0745. http://gold minesaloon.net. Cover $5. Map p 111.*

★ **Razzoo** FRENCH QUARTER   Hey Razzoo, Pat O's wants its flaming fountain back! Imitation is the sincerest form of flattery—and no one comes close to this club's dance floor, which is packed nightly with locals, students, and tourists shakin' their thing. *511 Bourbon St.* ☎ *504/522-5100. www.razzoo.com. No cover. Map p 111.*

Gay/Lesbian Bars

Bourbon Pub and Parade Disco FRENCH QUARTER   One of the country's largest gay clubs boasts a downstairs bar blaring dance music and videos 24/7, but if you have disco fever and an urge to dress up in tight, colorful costumes, head upstairs to show off the hustle, bus stop, four corners, the bump, and more classic moves. *801 Bourbon St.* ☎ *504/529-2107. www. bourbonpub.com. Cover $5–$10 weekends only. Map p 111.*

Café Lafitte in Exile FRENCH QUARTER   Former Lafitte's Blacksmith Shop owner Tom Caplinger opened this legendary gay gathering spot that drew Tennessee Williams as a regular; open 24 hours. *901 Bourbon St.* ☎ *504/522-8397. www.lafittes.com. No cover. Map p 111.*

Good Friends Bar FRENCH QUARTER   The attractive, friendly staff will make you feel at home and after a frozen Separator—brandy, milk, and coffee liqueur mixed with Kahlua ice cream—(or two), you'll want to join the group around the corner piano singing old favorites karaoke style. *740 Dauphine St.* ☎ *504/566-7191. www. goodfriendsbar.com. No cover. Map p 111.*

Le Roundup FRENCH QUARTER Drag queens, transsexuals, hot men, bad boys—they're all here and ready to party. If you're shy, you won't be for long. *819 St. Louis St.* ☎ *504/561-8340. Cover $2–$5. Map p 111.*

★★★ Oz FRENCH QUARTER Anything goes here among the hottest, most muscled, best-costumed men I've ever seen. They show off hip-swiveling moves that will make you blush or want to join in the naughty fun. *800 Bourbon St.* ☎ *504/ 593-9491. www.ozneworleans.com. Cover varies. Map p 111.*

Hip Spots

★★ Ampersand CENTRAL BUSINESS DISTRICT Housed in a former bank, Ampersand has plenty of room to groove on the giant dance floor. Or saunter over to a seat in the old vault that sets the tone for the club's cool industrial vibe and flashy European style. *1100 Tulane Ave.* ☎ *504/587-3737. www.club ampersand.com. Cover $10–$15. Map p 113.*

★★ The Circle Bar UPTOWN This old pink-and-white house is dwarfed by commercial buildings on either side, which adds to the feeling of just hanging out at a friend's place with 40 easygoing buddies. Intimate performances by singer-songwriters add to the coziness. *1032 St. Charles Ave. at Lee Circle.* ☎ *504/588-2616. www.circle barneworleans.com. No cover. Map p 113.*

d.b.a. FAUBOURG MARIGNY The New Orleans version of the popular NYC original feels spacious and homey, with a dark wood interior and dim lighting. Beer lovers should check out the long list of premium brews, including Belgian draft beer and hand-drawn ales. *618 Frenchmen St.* ☎ *504/942-3731. www.dbaneworleans.com. Cover $5–$10. Map p 114.*

★ The Dungeon FRENCH QUARTER I stupidly went here during Mardi Gras and was nearly crushed, which made it really feel like a claustrophobic dungeon. Dark and scary in a B-movie kind of way, it's a good choice for a late, late night (it doesn't open till midnight). *738 Toulouse St.* ☎ *504/523-5530. Cover $5. Map p 111.*

★ F&M Patio Bar UPTOWN Sure, the worn-down camelback house with some crazy additions on the back ain't much to look at, but inside everyone from coeds to working professionals is playing pool, swaying to classic rock, or crowding into the vintage photo booth so they can show off their black-and-white pics on the walls. *4841 Tchoupitoulas St.* ☎ *504/895-6784. No cover. Map p 112.*

★ One Eyed Jacks FRENCH QUARTER With a cool, cozy theater feel, this spot hosts everything from cabaret to comedy, plus Fast Times '80s Night (every Thurs). Its old-fashioned burlesque is miles away from the raunchiness of Bourbon Street. *615 Toulouse St.* ☎ *504/ 569-8361. www.oneeyedjacks.net. Cover $5–$15. Map p 111.*

★★ The Sazerac Bar FRENCH QUARTER The fab and posh Sazerac Bar, in the Roosevelt hotel, is named for its signature cocktail. The Ramos Gin Fizz and original

1930s Art Deco murals by artist Paul Ninas also make it worth a visit. *123 Baronne St.* ☎ *504/648-1200. No cover. Map p 111.*

Historic Bars

Lafitte's Blacksmith Shop Bar

FRENCH QUARTER You've found your perfect hangout if you like holing up in a dank, dark den (lit only by candles after sundown) among gregarious young locals. *941 Bourbon St.* ☎ *504/593-9761. No cover. Map p 111.*

★★★ Napoleon House

FRENCH QUARTER Stop in for the signature Pimm's Cup at this historic place with low-key lighting, strong drinks, and a relaxing atmosphere. *500 Chartres St.* ☎ *504/524-9752. www.napoleonhouse.com. No cover. Map p 111.*

The Old Absinthe House

FRENCH QUARTER Try the house specialty, the Absinthe House Frappe, which dates back to 1874. It still packs a punch even though the absinthe is now replaced with Herbsaint. *240 Bourbon St.* ☎ *504/523-3181. www.oldabsinthehouse.com. No cover. Map p 111.*

Old Absinthe House.

Jazz Clubs (Contemporary)

★ Irvin Mayfield's Jazz Playhouse

FRENCH QUARTER With the help of talented local jazz musicians like Germaine Bazzle, Jason Marsalis, Gerald French & the Original Tuxedo Band, New Orleans's own Grammy and Billboard award–winning Irvin Mayfield has succeeded in bringing some class back to Bourbon Street. *In the Royal Sonesta Hotel, 300 Bourbon St.* ☎ *504/586-0300. www.irvinmayfield.com. No cover. One-drink minimum. Map p 111.*

★★ Snug Harbor

FAUBOURG MARIGNY I've started many evenings enjoying the modern jazz interpretations of homegrown chanteuse Charmaine Neville (niece to Aaron), and you'd be wise to do the same. *626 Frenchmen St.* ☎ *504/949-0696. www.snugjazz.com. Cover $15–$40. Map p 114.*

Jazz Clubs (Traditional)

Fritzel's European Jazz Club

FRENCH QUARTER After a night of entertaining, jazz musicians gather here in the wee hours to jam and let off some steam. *733 Bourbon St.* ☎ *504/586-4800. www.fritzelsjazz.net. No cover. One-drink minimum per set. Map p 111.*

Maison Bourbon

FRENCH QUARTER Dixieland jazz attracts an older set of folks who are happy just tapping their toes to the oldies but goodies. *641 Bourbon St.* ☎ *504/522-8818. No cover. One-drink minimum. Map p 111.*

The Palm Court Jazz Café

FRENCH QUARTER During hot weather you might want to make reservations, because listening to old-fashioned jazz in air-conditioned comfort is priceless. Stick

Pat O'Brien's.

with drinks and pass on the expensive food. *1204 Decatur St.* ☎ *504/525-0200. www.palmcourtjazzcafe.com. Cover $5. Map p 111.*

★★ **Preservation Hall** FRENCH QUARTER This no-frills establishment is run by a nonprofit group dedicated to the preservation of jazz. *726 St. Peter St.* ☎ *888/946-JAZZ or* ☎ *504/522-2841. www.preservationhall.com. Cover $15. Map p 111.*

Karaoke
★ **Cat's Meow** FRENCH QUARTER If you have the urge to make a fool of yourself or watch others take a crack at classic radio songs ("Dream On," anyone?), you won't find a better place. *701 Bourbon St.* ☎ *504/523-2788. www.catskaraoke.com. Cover $5 under 21; no cover 21 and over. Map p 111.*

Piano Bars
★★★ **The Bombay Club** FRENCH QUARTER With a martini in hand—preferably the Breathless, made with SKYY vodka, white crème de cacao, and a splash of

Godiva liqueur in a chocolate-rimmed glass—lounge in the luxurious, elegant atmosphere. *In the Prince Conti Hotel, 830 Conti St.* ☎ *504/586-0972. www.thebombayclub.com. No cover. Map p 111.*

★★ **Carousel Revolving Bar** FRENCH QUARTER The slowly revolving bar is a whimsical detail in one of the city's more storied and immaculate historic hotels. *In the Hotel Monteleone, 214 Royal St.* ☎ *504/523-3341. www.hotelmonteleone.com. No cover. Map p 111.*

Feelings Café FAUBOURG MARIGNY Romantic yearnings are best expressed among the tropical plants and exposed brick of the intimate courtyard. Or you can sing to your beloved with backing by the piano player and the friendly patrons. *2600 Chartres St.* ☎ *504/945-2222. www.feelingscafe.com. No cover. Map p 114.*

Pat O'Brien's FRENCH QUARTER I'll admit it, the bar's world-famous Hurricane, a gigantic rum drink served in a hurricane lamp–style glass, is hard to resist, along with the flaming fountain and spacious courtyard. That said, you'll find nary a native. *718 St. Peter St.* ☎ *504/ 525-4823. www.patobriens.com. No cover. Map p 111.*

Pubs

Carrollton Station CARROLLTON A true (and tiny) neighborhood joint where old friends often meet and new folks are made to feel welcome. *8140 Willow St.* ☎ *504/865- 9190. Cover varies; no cover weekdays except during Jazz Fest. Map p 115.*

Cooter Brown's Tavern CARROLLTON Greasy cheese fries pair well with an astounding variety of domestic and international beers. *509 S. Carrollton Ave.* ☎ *504/866-9104. www.cooter browns.com. No cover. Map p 115.*

Kerry Irish Pub FRENCH QUARTER Enjoy a pint of Guinness while playing darts or pool, or just sit back and listen to live Irish or alternative folk music. *331 Decatur St.* ☎ *504/527-5954. www.kerryirishpub.com. No cover. Map p 111.*

Rock/Alternative Venues

Checkpoint Charlie's FRENCH QUARTER Rock out to up-and-coming bands in a typically smoky, dark dive with a young local crowd. *501 Esplanade Ave.* ☎ *504/281- 4847. No cover. Map p 111.*

★★ **The Howlin' Wolf** WAREHOUSE DISTRICT A hand-carved mahogany bar (it once belonged to Al Capone) and magnificent Michalopoulos mural set the stage for mainstream acts like (native son) Harry Connick, Jr., Alison Krauss, Jimmy Page, and the Barenaked Ladies. *907 S. Peters St.* ☎ *504/ 529-5844. www.thehowlinwolf.com. Cover varies. Map p 113.* ●

8 The Best Arts & Entertainment

Arts & Entertainment Best Bets

Best **Costumes**
Delta Festival Ballet, Dixon Hall, Tulane University, *Zimpel St. and Newcomb Place. (p 128)*

Best **High Note**
★★ New Orleans Opera Association, Mahalia Jackson Theatre, *1419 Basin St. (p 128)*

Best **Kid-Friendly Comedy**
La Nuit Comedy Theater, *5039 Freret St. (p 129)*

Best **Belly Laughs**
★ The National Comedy Company, the Shadowbox Theatre, *2400 St. Claude Ave. (p 129)*

Best **Place to Feel Your Stomach Drop**
Entergy IMAX Theatre, *1 Canal St. (p 129)*

Best **Nostalgic Night at the Movies**
★★★ The Prytania Theatre, *5339 Prytania St. (p 129)*

Best **Chance to Win Big**
★★ The Fair Grounds Race Course, *1751 Gentilly Blvd. (p 130)*

Best **Slam Dunk**
New Orleans Arena, *1501 Girod St. (p 131)*

Best **Stadium Crowd**
Mercedes-Benz Superdome, *1 Sugar Bowl Dr. (p 131)*

Best **Preshow Cocktail**
★★ Le Chat Noir, *715 St. Charles Ave. (p 131)*

Best **Use of a Stage**
★★★ Le Petit Théâtre, *616 St. Peter St. (p 132)*

Best **Culture Shock**
Zeitgeist Multi-Disciplinary Arts Center, *1618 Oretha Castle Haley Blvd. (p 132)*

Previous page: A performance at the Mahalia Jackson Theatre.
Below: Movie night at the Prytania Theatre.

French Quarter A & E

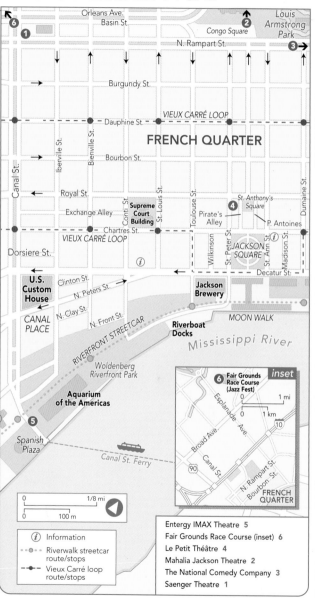

Entergy IMAX Theatre 5
Fair Grounds Race Course (inset) 6
Le Petit Théâtre 4
Mahalia Jackson Theatre 2
The National Comedy Company 3
Saenger Theatre 1

Central Business District A & E

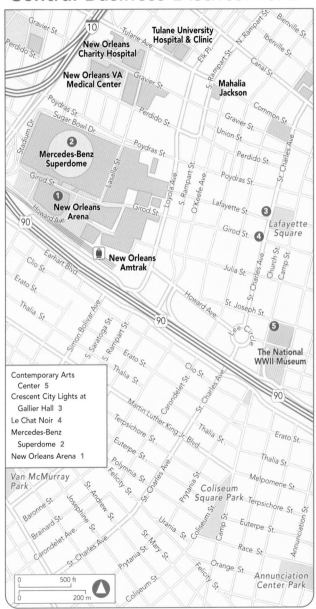

Contemporary Arts
    Center 5
Crescent City Lights at
    Gallier Hall 3
Le Chat Noir 4
Mercedes-Benz
    Superdome 2
New Orleans Arena 1

Uptown A & E

Delta Festival Ballet at Tulane University, Dixon Hall 1
La Nuit Comedy Theater 3
The Prytania Theatre 2
Zeitgeist Multi-Disciplinary Arts Center 4

Arts & Entertainment A to Z

Classical Music, Opera & Dance

kids Delta Festival Ballet
UPTOWN   The city's oldest professional ballet company showcases local talent. Its annual holiday production of *The Nutcracker* with the Louisiana Philharmonic Orchestra is hugely popular, especially with families. *Tulane University, Dixon Hall, plus other locations around the city.* ☎ *504/888-0931. www.delta festivalballet.com. Ticket prices vary. Map p 127.*

Louisiana Philharmonic Orchestra CENTRAL BUSINESS DISTRICT   Founded in 1991, the LPO is the only symphony in the nation whose musicians own and manage it. The season runs from September through May. *Mahalia Jackson Theatre, 1419 Basin St., plus other locations around the city.* ☎ *504/523-6530. www.lpomusic. com. Tickets start at $10. Map p 125.*

New Orleans Ballet Association CENTRAL BUSINESS DISTRICT   Entertaining and educating Southern dance aficionados since 1969, NOBA hosts dance troupes from around the world in lieu of having its own company. The season runs from October through May. *Mahalia Jackson Theatre, 1419 Basin St.* ☎ *504/522-0996. www.nobadance. com. Ticket prices vary. Map p 125.*

★★ New Orleans Opera Association CENTRAL BUSINESS DISTRICT   For more than 65 years, NOOA has presented classical opera pieces and more contemporary fare to appeal to younger audiences. *Mahalia Jackson Theatre, 1419 Basin St.* ☎ *800/881-4459 or 504/529-2278. www.neworleans opera.org. Ticket prices vary. Map p 125.*

Outside the Mahalia Jackson Theatre.

The Entergy IMAX Theatre is a great place to take the kids.

Comedy

kids La Nuit Comedy Theater

UPTOWN   New Orleans is renowned for its cast of eccentric characters, so it was just a matter of time before a smart, sassy improv company put down roots. Led by veteran comedian-actress Yvonne Landry, La Nuit also hosts the weeklong New Orleans Comedy Arts Festival every February. Kids of all ages are welcome at the clean-cut interactive performance "ComedySportz." *5039 Freret St.* ☎ *504/231-7011. www.nolacomedy. com. Tickets $5–$12; free open mic Fri night. Map p 127.*

★ The National Comedy Company FRENCH QUARTER   If you like *Whose Line Is It Anyway?* you'll love this Southern twist on the original. The audience calls the shots, and the comics—some of whom have performed with Ben Stein, Ryan Stiles, and David Cross—surprise you with their wacky spontaneity. You'll laugh so hard you'll cry. *Shadowbox Theatre, 2400 St. Claude Ave. (at St. Roch Ave.).* ☎ *504/523-7469. www.nationalcomedycompany. com. Tickets $8–$10. Map p 125.*

Film

kids Entergy IMAX Theatre

FRENCH QUARTER   Make the steep climb to your seat and prepare to feel like you're actually in the movie. (Seriously, I once got motion sickness watching a documentary on flying.) Everything from dinosaur science films to contemporary action flicks is presented on the giant screen. *1 Canal St.* ☎ *800/774-7394 or 504/581-4629. www.auduboninstitute.org/visit/imax. Tickets $8–$10.50. Map p 125.*

★★★ The Prytania Theatre

UPTOWN   This single-screen cinema is the city's oldest operating theater, and yet it's also completely digital, so you get the best of both worlds. Nonagenarian owner René Brunet will personally greet you at the door. I used to live right around the corner, so we were regular patrons, and I can still sing the '50s era "Let's All Go to the Lobby" snack-bar ad that precedes every film. Probably the strangest thing is asking for a ticket without having to say for which show. Film choices run the gamut, from classics to the latest blockbusters. *5339 Prytania*

The New Orleans Saints play at the Superdome.

St. ☎ 504/891-2787. www.the
prytania.com. Tickets $9.50–$11.50,
$5.75 before 6pm, add $3 for 3-D
movies. Map p 127.

Sports Venues
**★★ The Fair Grounds Race
Course** MID-CITY   The nation's
third-oldest horse-racing track has
tenaciously overcome fire, hurricanes, world wars, and the
Depression. The track and slots
attract die-hard gamblers, mon-
eyed socialites, and hooky-playing
coeds. The air-conditioned modern
clubhouse is fine, but my money is
always on the grandstand, where I
can feel the warm sun and see the
horses kick up dust as they charge
past. *1751 Gentilly Blvd.* ☎ *504/944-
5515. www.fairgroundsracecourse.
com. Tickets $10 clubhouse except*

The New Orleans Arena is the home court of the city's NBA team, the Pelicans.

$15 Ostrich and Zebra Racing, and Louisiana Derby Day; free grandstand except $5 Starlight Racing and Graded Stakes Day. Map p 125.

Mercedes-Benz Superdome
CENTRAL BUSINESS DISTRICT
Oh when the Saints go marchin' in…you will hear the crowd scream with excitement. The New Orleans Saints have the best fans around. The Superdome, their home, can hold 76,000 football fans or more than 100,000 concertgoers. Trade shows, conventions, and the annual Sugar Bowl also set up shop here. *1 Sugar Bowl Dr.* ☎ *504/587-3663. www.superdome.com. For Saints tickets, use NFL Ticket Exchange at www.nfl.com. Map p 126.*

New Orleans Arena CENTRAL
BUSINESS DISTRICT   The New Orleans Pelicans (formerly Hornets) basketball team continues to impress. Their new player, All-Star point guard Jrue Holiday, formerly of Philly, will no doubt be a fan favorite with his versatility and agility. *1501 Girod St.* ☎ *504/593-4999. www.neworleansarena.com. For Pelicans tickets, go to www.nba.com/pelicans. Map p 126.*

New Orleans Zephyrs Field
METAIRIE   Die-hard baseball fans root for the Zephyrs—the AAA farm team of the Houston Astros—in their spacious suburban stadium. *6000 Airline Dr., Metairie.* ☎ *504/734-5155. www.zephyrsbaseball.com. Tickets $1–$12.*

Theaters
★ Contemporary Arts Center
CENTRAL BUSINESS DISTRICT
This social hub attracts fans of modern art, experimental plays, dance productions, concerts, and the occasional film screening. The

Contemporary Arts Center.

rooms are small enough that every seat is a good one, although it can be a bit cramped when full. After the show, unwind with some coffee or wine at the Cyber Bar & Café. *900 Camp St.* ☎ *504/528-3805. www.cacno.org. Ticket prices vary. Map p 126.*

kids Crescent City Lights
CENTRAL BUSINESS DISTRICT
Supported by the New Orleans Recreation Department, CCL gives local children a chance to strut their stuff on stage. The summer production is usually kid-oriented, while the fall one is a better bet for adults. Musicals are the usual fare, and there's no dress code, so it's popular with families. *Gallier Hall, 545 St. Charles Ave.* ☎ *504/598-3800. www.crescentcitylights.com. Tickets $15. Map p 126.*

★★ Le Chat Noir CENTRAL
BUSINESS DISTRICT   Get dressed up and come early for a cocktail at the bar and stay for an experimental play, cabaret, or live music. *715 St. Charles Ave.* ☎ *504/581-5812. www.cabaretlechatnoir.com. Tickets free–$35. Map p 126.*

The "Stella" yelling contest at Le Petit Théâtre at the annual Tennessee Williams festival.

★★★ Le Petit Théâtre du Vieux Carré FRENCH QUARTER

Le Petit Théâtre is one of the oldest nonprofessional theater troupes in the U.S. The company presents everything from classic and contemporary plays and musicals to experimental fare from local writers. *616 St. Peter St. ☎ 504/522-2081. www.lepetittheatre.com. Tickets $35–$50. Map p 125.*

Saenger Theatre FRENCH QUARTER

Opened in 1927 at a cost of $2.5 million, the venerable Saenger is listed on the National Register of Historic Places. The interior resembles an Italian courtyard, complete with a "starry" sky of 150 small lights formed into constellations. There are few better places to see top acts ranging from Jerry Seinfeld to Diana Ross. *1111 Canal St. ☎ 504/257-0351. www.saengernola.com. Map p 125.*

Southern Rep Theatre FRENCH QUARTER

New Southern plays are showcased by casts that include a mix of green young actors and experienced local talent. *Contemporary Arts Center, 900 Camp St. ☎ 504/522-6545. www.southernrep. com. Tickets $25–$35. Map p 126.*

Zeitgeist Multi-Disciplinary Arts Center UPTOWN

Come here with an open mind; this is not your grandma's theater! The people-watching is just as fascinating as the experimental shows. For safety's sake, please take a cab. *1618 Oretha Castle Haley Blvd. ☎ 504/352-1150. www.zeitgeistinc. net. Tickets $6–$8. Map p 127.* ●

Lodging Best Bets

Most **Luxurious**
★★★ Ritz-Carlton $$$
921 Canal St. (p 145)

Best **Views**
★ Omni Royal Orleans $$
621 St. Louis St. (p 144)

Most **Exclusive Hotel**
★★★ Le Pavillon Hotel $
833 Poydras St. (p 143)

Most **Historic**
★★★ Hotel Monteleone $$
214 Royal St. (p 142)

Hippest **Hotel**
★ W French Quarter $$$
316 Chartres St. (p 146)

Best **French Quarter Hotel**
★ Bourbon Orleans Hotel $$
717 Orleans St. (p 139)

Best **Moderately Priced Hotel**
★ Bienville House $$–$$$
320 Decatur St. (p 139)

Best **Bathrooms**
★★ McKendrick-Breaux House $$
1474 Magazine St. (p 144)

Best **Family Hotel**
★ Holiday Inn–Chateau LeMoyne
$$ *301 Dauphine St. (p 141)*

Best **Cheap Bed**
★★ St. Vincent's Guest House $
1507 Magazine St. (p 145)

Most **Romantic**
★★ Soniat House $$
1133 Chartres St. (p 146)

Best **Boutique Hotel**
★★★ International House $$
221 Camp St. (p 142)

Best **Bed & Breakfast**
★ Grand Victorian Bed &
Breakfast $$ *2727 St. Charles Ave.
(p 141)*

Previous page: The lobby of the Hotel Monteleone.
Below: A luxurious room at the Ritz-Carlton.

Uptown/Mid-City Lodging

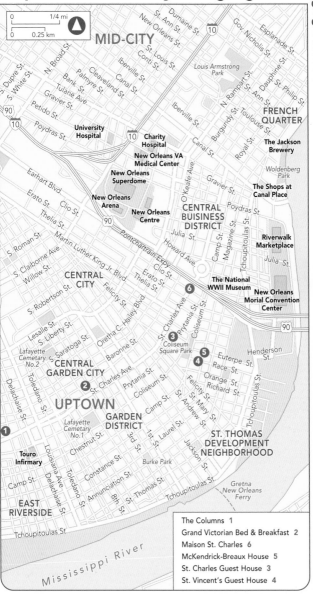

The Columns 1
Grand Victorian Bed & Breakfast 2
Maison St. Charles 6
McKendrick-Breaux House 5
St. Charles Guest House 3
St. Vincent's Guest House 4

French Quarter & Faubourg

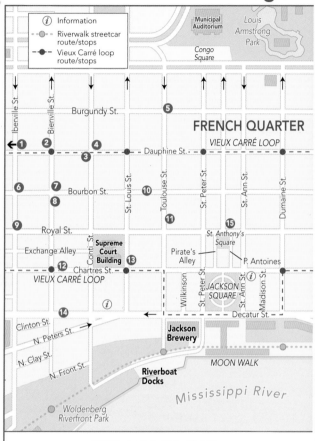

B&W Courtyards Bed & Breakfast 24
Bienville House 14
Bourbon Orleans Hotel 15
Chateau Bourbon – Wyndham Historic Hotel 6
Chateau Hotel 17
Dauphine Orleans Hotel 4
The Frenchmen Hotel 23
Four Points by Sheraton 10
Holiday Inn-Chateau LeMoyne 2
Hotel Maison de Ville 11
The Hotel Mazarin 8
Hotel Monteleone 9
Hotel Provincial 18

Marigny Lodging

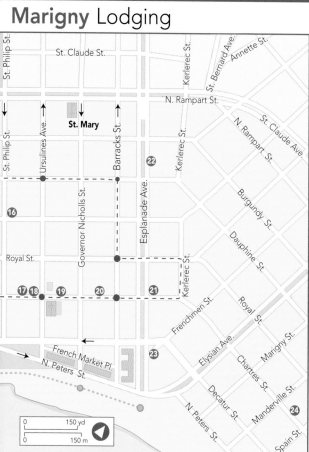

St. Philip St.

St. Claude St.

Kerlerec St.

St. Bernard Ave.

Annette St.

N. Rampart St.

St. Philip St.

Ursulines Ave.

St. Mary

Barracks St.

Kerlerec St.

N. Rampart St.

St. Claude Ave.

16

Governor Nicholls St.

Esplanade Ave.

22

Kerlerec St.

Burgundy St.

Dauphine St.

Royal St.

17 **18** **19** **20** **21**

Frenchmen St.

Royal St.

Marigny St.

23

Elysian Ave.

Chartres St.

French Market Pl.

N. Peters St.

Decatur St.

Manderville St.

N. Peters St.

24

Spain St.

0 — 150 yd
0 — 150 m

Lafitte Guest House **16**
Lamothe House **21**
Le Richelieu Hotel **20**
Maison Dupuy **5**
Melrose Mansion **22**
Omni Royal Orleans **13**
Prince Conti Hotel **3**
Ritz-Carlton New Orleans **1**
Royal Sonesta **7**
Soniat House **19**
W French Quarter **12**

Central Business District Lodging

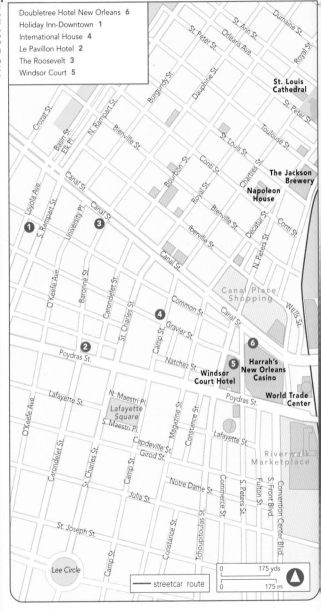

Doubletree Hotel New Orleans **6**
Holiday Inn-Downtown **1**
International House **4**
Le Pavillon Hotel **2**
The Roosevelt **3**
Windsor Court **5**

St. Louis
Cathedral

The Jackson
Brewery

Napoleon
House

Canal Place
Shopping

Harrah's
New Orleans
Casino

Windsor
Court Hotel

World Trade
Center

Lafayette
Square

Riverwalk
Marketplace

Lee Circle

streetcar route

0   175 yds
0   175 m

Lodging A to Z

B&W Courtyards Bed & Breakfast FAUBOURG MARIGNY Most of the uniquely decorated guest rooms open onto a quiet courtyard. Your best bet is the former slave quarters, converted into a private tropical retreat. *2425 Chartres St.* ☎ *800/585-5731 or 504/945-9418. www.bandwcourtyards.com. 6 units. Doubles $99–$250. AE, DISC, MC, V. Map p 136.*

★ Bienville House FRENCH QUARTER The classically elegant interior features hand-painted wall murals. Some rooms have a wrought-iron balcony with a view of the flagstone courtyard. There's also a saltwater pool. *320 Decatur St.* ☎ *800/535-7836 or 504/529-2345. www.bienvillehouse.com. 83 units. Doubles $99–$189. AE, DC, DISC, MC, V. Map p 136.*

★ kids Bourbon Orleans Hotel FRENCH QUARTER This lavish hotel has got it all: location, history, and good service. Rooms on the Royal Street side are less noisy.

Kids will enjoy the outdoor pool and can sleep on pullout sofas in the bi-level suites. *717 Orleans St.* ☎ *866/513-9744 or 504/523-2222. www.bourbonorleans.com. 218 units. Doubles $139–$329. AE, DC, DISC, MC, V. Map p 136.*

Chateau Bourbon–Wyndham Historic Hotel FRENCH QUARTER Located in the late-19th-century D. H. Holmes Department Store building, the Chateau Bourbon's rooms (large, though nonspecific in style or charm) benefited from a post-Katrina makeover. A statue of Ignatius Reilly, the protagonist of the Pulitzer Prize–winning novel *A Confederacy of Dunces,* greets visitors at the hotel's Canal Street entrance. *800 Iberville St.* ☎ *877/999-3223 or 504/586-0800. www.chateaubourbonneworleans.com. 251 units. Doubles $99–$350. AE, DC, DISC, MC, V. Map p 136.*

Chateau Hotel FRENCH QUARTER A good deal in a good location, the Chateau offers European charm and some peace and

The elegant lobby at Bourbon Orleans Hotel.

The Columns was featured in an Alicia Keys music video.

quiet just a stone's throw from busy Bourbon Street. The rooms are clean and feature antique furnishings. *1001 Chartres St.* ☎ *504/524-9636. www.chateauhotel.com. 45 units. Doubles $89–$159. AE, DC, MC, V. Map p 136.*

★★ The Columns UPTOWN
The rooms are cozy, and the dining area is worn in a well-loved way, but the real draw is sipping drinks on the huge, shady porch while listening to locals gossip and the streetcars rattle by. You may recognize this site as the setting for Louis Malle's film about Storyville, *Pretty Baby. 3811 St. Charles Ave.* ☎ *800/445-9308 or 504/899-9308. www.the columns.com. 19 units. Doubles $160–$230; summer rates $99–$173. AE, MC, V. Map p 135.*

kids Dauphine Orleans Hotel
FRENCH QUARTER Stay here for the perfect combo of vintage charm and modern perks. The multiple lovely private courtyards are also a draw. John James Audubon used the rear of the building as a studio. *415 Dauphine St.* ☎ *800/521-7111 or 504/586-1800. www.dauphineorleans.com. 111 units. Doubles $99–$299. AE, DC, DISC, MC, V. Map p 136.*

kids Doubletree Hotel New Orleans CENTRAL BUSINESS DISTRICT Expect the usual from this clean, comfortable chain hotel. Decent-size rooms and a laid-back atmosphere are a plus for families. At check-in, the kids get chocolate-chip cookies, plus who wouldn't love a rooftop pool? *300 Canal St.* ☎ *888/874-9074 or 504/581-1300. www.doubletree.com. 550 units. Doubles $79–$229. AE, DC, DISC, MC, V. Map p 138.*

Four Points by Sheraton Hotel
FRENCH QUARTER This hotel stands on the site of the French Opera House, which burned to the ground in 1919. But the spot is better known for its coveted rooms with balconies for hard-core Mardi Gras revelers. *541 Bourbon St.* ☎ *866/716-8133 or 504/524-7611. www.fourpointsfrenchquarter.com. 186 units. Doubles $109–$159. AE, DISC, MC, V. Map p 136.*

The Frenchmen Hotel FAU-BOURG MARIGNY Typical of the 1860s, the rooms in these adjoining historic Creole town houses are teeny, but you'll probably spend most of your time in the pool or hot tub in the brick courtyard anyway. *417 Frenchmen St.* ☎ *800/831-1781* or 504/948-2166. www.frenchmen hotel.com. 27 units. Doubles $59–$250. AE, DISC, MC, V. Map p 136.

★ Grand Victorian Bed & Breakfast UPTOWN

This gorgeous 1893 home has been transformed into the grandest B&B on the avenue. Expect elegantly furnished rooms and some baths with Jacuzzi tubs. 2727 St. Charles Ave. ☎ 800/977-0008 or 504/895-1104. www.gvbb.com. 8 units. Doubles $165–$235. AE, DISC, MC, V. Map p 135.

★ kids Holiday Inn–Chateau LeMoyne FRENCH QUARTER

Not bad for a chain, featuring comfortable, albeit bland, rooms and convenient walking distance to family-friendly attractions. 301 Dauphine St. ☎ 800/HOLIDAY or 504/581-1303. www.chateaulemoyne frenchquarter.com. 171 units. Doubles $89–$339. AE, DC, DISC, MC, V. Map p 136.

Holiday Inn–Downtown CENTRAL BUSINESS DISTRICT

You'll find clean, good-size rooms here, typical of the Holiday Inn chain. Sports fans like the proximity to the Superdome and New Orleans Arena for football and basketball, respectively. It's also a popular choice for Essence Fest. 330 Loyola Ave. ☎ 800/535-7830 or 504/581-1600. www.hi-neworleans.com. 500 units. Doubles $120–$230. Children 18 and under free in parent's room. AE, DC, DISC, MC, V. Map p 138.

Hotel Maison de Ville FRENCH QUARTER

The Bourbon Street side of this atmospheric and romantic hotel (Tennessee Williams was a frequent guest) can be noisy, so be sure to inquire about room location when booking. The best night's sleep can be had in one of the charming Audubon Cottages. 727 Toulouse St. ☎ 504/324-4888. www.maisondeville.com. 18 units. Doubles $210–$299. AE, DC, MC, V. Map p 136.

Hotel Mazarin FRENCH QUARTER

Pamper yourself with in-room spa services, a signature St. Germain cocktail at Patrick's Bar Vin, and the serene sounds of the old-world fountain in the tranquil Mediterranean courtyard. 730 Bienville St. ☎ 800/535-9111 or 504/581-7300. www.hotelmazarin.com. 102 units. Doubles $79–$189. AE, DISC, MC, V. Map p 136.

Grand Victorian Bed & Breakfast.

The rooftop pool at the Hotel Monteleone.

★★★ Hotel Monteleone

FRENCH QUARTER One dizzying look at the revolving Carousel Bar and the luxurious lobby and you'll know why literary lions like William Faulkner, Richard Ford, Ernest Hemingway, Rebecca Wells, Eudora Welty, and Tennessee Williams stayed here. A basic room can be small, so go for a two-room suite if you want to stretch out. Be sure to enjoy the rooftop pool. *214 Royal St. ☎ 866/338-4684 or 504/523-3341. www.hotelmonteleone.com. 600 units. Doubles $229–$339. Children under 18 stay free in their parent's room. AE, DC, DISC, MC, V. Map p 136.*

Hotel Provincial

FRENCH QUARTER Run by the Dupepe family since 1969, this luxurious hotel—complete with high ceilings

The Petite Suite at the Hotel Provincial.

and French and Creole antiques— once housed a Civil War hospital. You'd never know. *1024 Chartres St. ☎ 800/535-7922 or 504/581-4995. www.hotelprovincial.com. 92 units. Doubles $79–$289. AE, DC, DISC, MC, V. Map p 136.*

★★★ International House

CENTRAL BUSINESS DISTRICT This sensual, state-of-the-art sanctuary showcases the European, African, and Caribbean heritage of the city. A top-of-the-line modern hotel, the International House attracts media types and other travelers looking for a sophisticated stay. *221 Camp St. ☎ 800/633-5770 or 504/553-9550. www.ihhotel.com. 117 units. Doubles $119–$379. AE, DC, MC, V. Map p 138.*

Lafitte Guest House

FRENCH QUARTER Built in 1849, the three-story brick mansion features wrought-iron balconies, Victorian flair, and pralines on the pillows. Guests are invited to socialize over wine and cheese in the parlor every afternoon. *1003 Bourbon St. ☎ 800/331-7971 or 504/581-2678. www.lafitteguesthouse.com. 14 units. Doubles $159–$229. AE, DC, DISC, MC, V. Map p 136.*

Lamothe House

FRENCH QUARTER This is a place for the unfussy

Lafitte Guest House is rumored to be haunted.

traveler who prefers a lived-in homey look where you can put your feet up on the coffee table. A courtyard with banana trees offers a quiet respite. *621 Esplanade Ave. ☎ 800/367-5858 or 504/947-1161. www.frenchquarterguesthouses.com. 35 units. Doubles $69–$199. AE, DISC, MC, V. Map p 136.*

★★★ Le Pavillon Hotel CENTRAL BUSINESS DISTRICT
Extravagance, thy name is Le Pavillon. The soaring lobby's crystal chandeliers, Oriental rugs, and rich oil paintings serve as the backdrop for signature peanut-butter-and-jelly sandwiches served on a silver platter with chocolates and milk nightly. This combination of whimsy and elegance is what makes Le Pavillon such a special place to stay. *833 Poydras St. ☎ 800/535-9095 or 504/581-3111. www.lepavillon.com. 226 units. Doubles $149–$319. AE, DC, DISC, MC, V. Map p 138.*

kids Le Richelieu Hotel FRENCH QUARTER
Paul McCartney and his late wife, Linda, stayed here

The sleek, sophisticated lobby of the International House.

with their kids back in the day when he was working on a Wings album. Despite the old-world charm and celebrity appeal, the convenient location and pool still make it a kid-friendly choice. *1234 Chartres St. ☎ 800/535-9653 or 504/529-2492. www.lerichelieuhotel.com. 86 units. Doubles $95–$180. AE, DC, DISC, MC, V. Map p 136.*

kids Maison Dupuy FRENCH QUARTER
A picturesque luxury hotel with impeccable service, Maison Dupuy is within walking distance of Bourbon Street, but far enough away to boast quiet rooms for a good night's sleep. If you want a balcony, be sure to ask if it's semiprivate first. This was once the site of the first cotton press in the U.S. *1001 Toulouse St. ☎ 800/535-9177 or 504/586-8000. www.maison dupuy.com. 200 units. Doubles $99–$269. AE, DC, DISC, MC, V. Map p 136.*

★ Maison St. Charles LOWER GARDEN DISTRICT
This inn comprises five large antebellum town homes and some newer construction, which makes for an eclectic mix of rooms, plus a tropical courtyard and pool. For safety, stick close to the avenue. *1319 St. Charles Ave. ☎ 504/522-0187. www.maisonstcharles.com. 165 units. Doubles $89–$189. Map p 135.*

A sweet shady spot at the McKendrick-Breaux House.

★★ McKendrick-Breaux House

LOWER GARDEN DISTRICT A spacious Greek Revival mansion in a hip neighborhood with plenty of restaurants and shops, McKendrick-Breaux House offers atmospheric antiques-filled rooms with artwork by local artists. *1474 Magazine St.* ☎ *888/570-1700 or 504/586-1700. www.mckendrick-breaux.com. 9 units. Doubles $145–$245. AE, MC, V. Map p 135.*

Melrose Mansion FAUBOURG

MARIGNY This meticulously restored historic home has tasteful Victorian decor (no flowery wallpaper here) in its well-maintained and roomy accommodations. *937 Esplanade Ave.* ☎ *800/650-3323*

or 504/944-2255. www.frenchquarter hotelgroup.com. 15 units. Doubles $125–$269. AE, DISC, MC, V. Map p 136.

★ kids Omni Royal Orleans

FRENCH QUARTER An elegant member of the Omni chain, this location is popular with parents because of its inexpensive babysitting service and proximity to museums and parks. Request a room with double beds or a rollaway bed for the kids. *621 St. Louis St.* ☎ *800/THE-OMNI [843-6664] or 504/529-5333. www.omniroyal orleans.com. 346 units. Doubles $189–$339. Children 17 and under free with parent. AE, DC, DISC, MC, V. Map p 136.*

Prince Conti Hotel FRENCH

QUARTER This is a great choice if you're looking for a reasonably priced, clean room and don't mind the lack of upscale amenities such as a pool and courtyard. It's all good . . . well, except for the tiny bathrooms. Stop by the Bombay Club for the best martinis in town (see p 136). *830 Conti St.* ☎ *800/ 366-2743 or 504/529-4172. www. princecontihotel.com. 76 units. Doubles $51–$206. AE, DC, DISC, MC, V. Map p 136.*

Inside the Melrose Mansion.

The famous Sazerac Bar at the Roosevelt hotel.

★★★ Ritz-Carlton New Orleans FRENCH QUARTER

Louisiana's only AAA Five Diamond luxury hotel underwent an extravagant post-Katrina renovation that re-creates the ambience of a magnificent antebellum mansion but still offers modern amenities and service. A world-class spa and fine restaurant make it easy to indulge. *921 Canal St.* ☎ *800/241-3333 or 504/524-1331. www.ritzcarlton.com. 452 units. Doubles $199–$349. AE, DISC, MC, V. Map p 137.*

★★★ kids The Roosevelt

CENTRAL BUSINESS DISTRICT The timelessly elegant hotel (formerly the Fairmont) where the likes of Bill Clinton and Huey Long stayed offers amenities such as the renowned Sazerac Bar and Restaurant, a rooftop pool, a workout area, and a spa. A winter wonderland lobby display during the holidays entertains children of all ages. *123 Baronne St.* ☎ *800/WALDORF or 504/648-1200. www.theroosevelt neworleans.com. 504 units. Doubles $159–$499. AE, DC, DISC, MC, V. Map p 138.*

Royal Sonesta FRENCH QUARTER Bourbon Street action dressed up in a classy package. For a good night's sleep, ask for an inside-facing room. *300 Bourbon St.* ☎ *800/ SONESTA or 504/586-0300. www. sonesta.com. 483 units. Doubles $109–$329. AE, DC, DISC, MC, V. Map p 136.*

★ St. Charles Guest House

LOWER GARDEN DISTRICT This no-frills funky place appeals to college kids and adventure seekers who just need a place to catch some zzz's. The rooms don't have phones (and some have no air-conditioning), but there is a lovely little courtyard with a swimming pool. *1748 Prytania St.* ☎ *504/523-6556. www.stcharlesguesthouse.com. 26 units. Doubles $45–$95. AE, MC, V. Map p 135.*

★★ St. Vincent's Guest House

LOWER GARDEN DISTRICT Once an orphanage, this early-20th-century brick building has been transformed into an extraordinarily affordable place to stay (some hostel-style accommodations available). It doesn't skimp on

A charming sitting area at Soniat House.

atmosphere, service, or amenities. *1507 Magazine St.* ☎ *504/302-9606. www.stvguesthouse.com. 70 units. Hostel $25 per person, doubles $45–$89. AE, DC, DISC, MC, V. Map p 135.*

★★ **Soniat House** FRENCH QUARTER   With an opulent plantation-era atmosphere, the Soniat

High-end luxury at the Windsor Court hotel.

House offers fine French and English antiques and Oriental rugs, but the bathrooms are small. See p 136. *1133 Chartres St.* ☎ *800/544-8808 or 504/522-0570. www.soniat house.com. 31 units. Doubles $195–$325. Children under 10 not permitted. AE, MC, V. Map p 136.*

★ **W French Quarter** FRENCH QUARTER   This superchic contemporary hotel attracts mostly young professionals. Locals eat up the Italian/Creole cuisine at in-house Bacco. *316 Chartres St.* ☎ *800/627-8260 or 504/581-1200. www.whotels. com. 98 units. Doubles $209–$509. AE, DC, DISC, MC, V. Map p 136.*

★★★ **Windsor Court** CENTRAL BUSINESS DISTRICT   You get what you pay for here—excellent service, large suites, and all the high-end amenities you could possibly want. *300 Gravier St.* ☎ *888/596-0955 or 504/523-6000. www. windsorcourthotel.com. 322 units. Doubles $195–$440. Children 16 and under free in parent's room. AE, DC, DISC, MC, V. Map p 138.* ●

Cajun Country

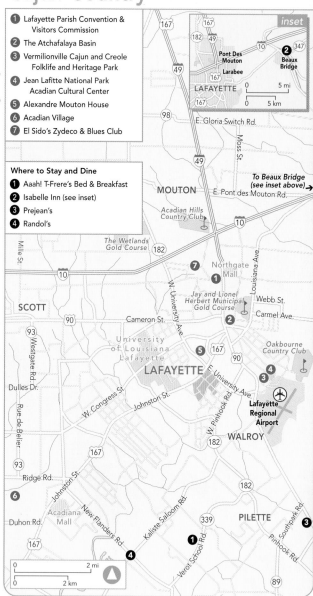

1. Lafayette Parish Convention & Visitors Commission
2. The Atchafalaya Basin
3. Vermilionville Cajun and Creole Folklife and Heritage Park
4. Jean Lafitte National Park Acadian Cultural Center
5. Alexandre Mouton House
6. Acadian Village
7. El Sido's Zydeco & Blues Club

Where to Stay and Dine

1. Aaah! T-Frere's Bed & Breakfast
2. Isabelle Inn (see inset)
3. Prejean's
4. Randol's

Previous page: A group tours the Barataria Preserve outside Lafitte.

Cajuns have influenced Louisiana cooking, music, and language since their Acadian ancestors were deported from a colony in Nova Scotia more than 300 years ago. The French-speaking people moved to southern Louisiana, which was under control of France at the time. They settled unwanted swampland, isolated but free to create their own way of life and culture. Despite modern pressures to conform, the Cajun community remains strong, particularly in Lafayette, just a few hours from New Orleans. START: **Head west on Interstate 10 from New Orleans. Lafayette, your first stop, is about 135 miles (217km) away, a 2.5-hour drive.**

A bird in Atchafalaya Basin swamp.

① The Lafayette Parish Convention and Visitors Commission. This is the perfect place to stop and plan your day with the help of friendly staff, brochures, and maps. Feel free to ask about the city's combination of Cajun, Caribbean, French, and Spanish influences, making it one of the world's most unique cultures. *1400 NW Evangeline Thruway, Lafayette.* ☎ *800/346-1958 or 337/232-3737. www.lafayettetravel. com. Weekdays 8:30am–5pm, weekends 9am–5pm.*

Head south on NW Evangeline Thruway, turn left at Dudley Avenue, then right at NW Evangeline Thruway/US-167. Turn left on Mudd Avenue/US-90 and turn

right on N. Sterling Street (1 mile/1.6km, 3 min.).

② The Atchafalaya Experience. The Atchafalaya Basin is the largest river swamp in the U.S. and home to abundant fish, birds (some endangered), and other wildlife. Environmentally conscious father-son guides Coerte A. Voorhies, Jr., a semiretired geologist, and Kim B. Voorhies, an avid hunter/fisherman, are extremely knowledgeable about the area's delicate and varied ecosystems and southern Louisiana culture in general. *338 N. Sterling St., Lafayette.* ☎ *337/277-4726. www. theatchafalayaexperience.com. Tours by appointment only. Call for fares (depends on length of boat ride and what you want to see). Departures twice daily, weather permitting.*

Head south on N. Sterling Street then left on E. Simcoe Street. Turn right at Surrey Street then right again at Fisher Road (2 miles/3.2km, 7 min.).

③ kids Vermilionville Cajun and Creole Folklife and Heritage Park. Perhaps a bit Disney-fied, with its costumed dancing Cajuns, it's still a fun way to explore a unique American culture. *300 Fisher Rd., Lafayette.* ☎ *866/99-BAYOU (992-2968) or 337/233-4077. www.vermilionville.org. Admission $10 adults, $8 seniors, $6 children 6–18, free children 5 and under. Tues–Sun 10am–4pm.*

A display at Jean Lafitte National Park Acadian Cultural Center.

Go 2 blocks southeast on Fisher Road.

④ kids Jean Lafitte National Park Acadian Cultural Center. Learn how the Acadian people were exiled from Nova Scotia and settled in the swamps of southern Louisiana, where their isolation fostered a unique way of life. *501 Fisher Rd., Lafayette.* ☎ *337/232-0789. www.nps.gov/Jela. Free admission; donations welcome. Tues–Sat 9:30am–4pm.*

Head east on Fisher Road then turn right on Surrey Street. Continue on E. University Avenue. Turn right at Lafayette Street.

⑤ Alexandre Mouton House. This elegant antebellum home on the National Register of Historic Places was originally built for Vermilionville founder Jean Mouton. It now houses the Lafayette

Museum's collection of Acadian history and culture. *1122 Lafayette St., Lafayette.* ☎ *337/234-2208. Admission $3 adults, $2 seniors, $1 children. Tues–Sat 10am–4pm.*

Head south on Lafayette Street. Turn left at LA-182/W. University Avenue, then right at Johnston Street/US-167 and continue for 5½ miles (8.7km). Turn right at Duhon Road/LA-342, right at W. Broussard Road, right at New Hope Road, then left at Greenleaf Drive.

⑥ kids Acadian Village. This "folklife museum" depicts an authentic 19th-century Cajun bayou community. The cute gift shop sells handmade Cajun crafts and books. *200 Greenleaf Dr., Lafayette.* ☎ *800/962-9133 or 337/981-2364. www.acadianvillage.org. Admission $8 adults, $7 seniors, $6 children 5–17, free children 4 and under. Tues–Sat 10am–4pm.*

⑦ El Sido's Zydeco & Blues Club. This plain commercial building comes alive with funky music guaranteed to get you on the dance floor. Respected local zydeco and Cajun musicians are known to stop by and share the stage. *1523 N. St. Antoine St., Lafayette.* ☎ *337/237-1959. Cover $8. Fri–Sat 9pm–2am, occasionally Sun–Mon during festival weekends.*

Where to Stay & Dine

Lodging
★★ Aaah! T-Frere's Bed & Breakfast. If you have a sense of humor, you'll love the funny family that runs this comfortable inn. Former chef Maugie Pastor serves delicious full breakfasts with whimsical names like "Ooh La La, Mardi Gras" while dressed in bright red

silk pajamas. My favorite unit is the Mary Room, for its huge antique bed and less-frilly decor (most rooms here have a country-Victorian scheme). *1905 Verot School Rd., Lafayette.* ☎ *800/984-9347 or 337/984-9347. www.tfreres.com. 8 units. Doubles $135 w/breakfast. AE, DC, DISC, MC, V.*

At the Acadian Village.

★ **kids Isabelle Inn.** Just 15 minutes outside Lafayette, this spacious home is well worth the drive. The Richard Room is beautifully appointed with antiques and offers a gorgeous view from the balcony. I also like the serene cottage feel of the Allison Room. Unlike at most B&Bs, kids are welcome and will love the pool and exploring the garden. *1130 Berard St., Breaux Bridge.* ☎ *337/412-0455. www. isabelleinn.com. 5 units. Doubles $175–$195. AE, MC, V.*

Dining

★★★ **kids Prejean's.** All things Cajun greet you as soon as you step inside, including the photo-op-friendly 14-foot (4.2m) taxidermy alligator Big Al, posed in the middle of the swamp-themed dining room. Get all your favorites on one plate—its signature seafood platter features fried frog legs, shrimp, oysters, catfish, alligator, stuffed shrimp, and stuffed crab, and is served with spicy sides like dirty rice or corn *maque choux.* Live Cajun music nightly. *3480 NE Evangeline Thruway (I-49), Lafayette.* ☎ *337/896-3247. www.prejeans. com. Reservations recommended. Entrees $17–$30. AE, DC, DISC, MC, V. Breakfast, lunch & dinner daily.*

Randol's. Owner Frank Randol fosters a community spirit here, based on gathering to eat good, simple food and dance the night away. Indulge in the cheesy, gooey Louisiana crawfish enchiladas then work off those calories on the dance floor. Locals will show you all the right moves. *2320 Kaliste Saloom Rd., Lafayette.* ☎ *800/962-2586 or 337/981-7080. www.randols. com. Entrees $14–$27. MC, V. Dinner served Sun–Thurs 5–9:30pm, Fri–Sat 5–10:30pm.*

The dance floor at Randol's.

Lafitte

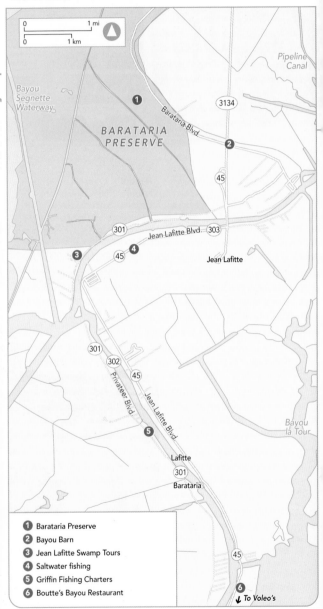

1 Barataria Preserve
2 Bayou Barn
3 Jean Lafitte Swamp Tours
4 Saltwater fishing
5 Griffin Fishing Charters
6 Boutte's Bayou Restaurant

↓ To Voleo's

Lafitte is an intriguing small town where many people still fish for a living and wealthy New Orleanians build sprawling country homes. When the cityscape seems too hurried and crowded, we escape here to the natural beauty and open water of our favorite shrimping village. Despite the threats of hurricane flooding and encroaching development, local tradition lives on. START: **From New Orleans, take Interstate 10 east, toward the Mississippi River. Cross the Crescent City Connection, and continue on what becomes the West Bank Expressway (yes, you're headed east, but it's the west side of the river bank). Exit at 4B Barataria Boulevard. Turn left at the second stoplight, onto Barataria Boulevard, then turn left on Leo Kerner/Lafitte Parkway.**

❶ The Barataria Preserve. This preserve offers hiking, fishing, and canoeing along freshwater marshlands and sleepy bayous. There are plenty of prime bird-watching opportunities. Remember mosquito repellent! *Visitor center, 6488 Barataria Blvd., Marrero.* ☎ *504/589-2133. www.nps.gov/jela/barataria-preserve. htm. Free admission, donations welcome. Trails open daily 7am–dusk, visitor center open Wed–Sun 9:30am–4:30pm.*

Head southwest on Barataria Blvd/ LA-301.

❷ Bayou Barn. It's not unusual for a local establishment to be all things to all people. Bayou Barn is a rustic open-air "restaurant" (think picnic tables under a roof) that packs in the crowds for its weekly Sunday Cajun dances. During the

day, it rents out canoes for exploring beautiful Bayou des Familles. Just beware of the large alligator gar fish that rest below the surface. Take my word for it: you do not want to bop one on the head with your paddle! Rentals must be returned by dark. *7145 Barataria Blvd., Crown Point.* ☎ *800/862-2968 or 504/689-2663. www.bayoubarn. com. Canoe rentals $20/hr. Mon–Fri 10am–5pm, Sat–Sun 10am–8pm.*

Head west on Barataria Blvd/ LA-45 N. Take first right onto Leo Kerner Lafitte Parkway/LA-3134 N.

❸ kids Jean Lafitte Swamp Tours. Local Cajun tour guides shares stories about the legendary pirate Jean Lafitte and the native way of life. Kids will enjoy sightings of fish, egrets, nutria, mink, snakes, and of course, alligators. *6601 Leo*

The lush Barataria Preserve.

Bayou Barn canoes.

Kerner Lafitte Parkway, Marrero. ☎ *800/445-4109. www.jeanlafitte swamptour.com. Admission $25 adults, $13 children 4–12, and free children 2 and under. Call for tour times.*

Lafitte's swamps and bayous are home to pelicans, alligators, shrimp, and crawfish.

Head south on Sunrise Dr/LA-3134 S. Turn left onto Jean Lafitte Blvd/ LA-303/LA-45. Destination will be on right.

4 Saltwater fishing. Captain Phil Robichaux or a member of his professional fishing-charter team can help you find where the redfish and speckled trout are lurking. The price includes all terminal tackle, artificial baits, gas, oil, ice, fish cleaning, and rods and reels. Customers must provide their own beverages, food, and fishing license. Fishing licenses are required by the State of Louisiana Department of Wildlife and Fisheries and are available for purchase online or by phone (www.wlf.state.la.us; ☎ 888/ 765-2602). Fishing permits cost $9.50 (annual) resident, $5 (1 day) or $15 (4 days) nonresident, plus service fee if ordered online/by phone. *1842 Jean Lafitte Blvd., Lafitte.* ☎ *504/689-2006. www.fishwithphil. com. Departures daily 6–6:30am, return 1:30–2:30pm.*

Where to Stay & Dine

This is the kind of small town with colorful characters that you'd think only exists in movies or books. It's definitely worth staying a day or two more to mingle with the locals

Lodging

Griffin Fishing Tours & Charters. Owners James and Rosemary Arcediano provide everything fish-loving families could want. Fish off the private docks or take a guided tour of the brackish Barataria waterways to catch plentiful redfish, speckled trout, flounder, bass, and more. Guides will prepare your catch for dockside lunches or dinner with fellow guests at its own Cajun Cook House. Cabins and camp quarters are comfy and rustic, decorated with the avid outdoorsman in mind. Golf and horseshoes are also available. *2629 Privateer Blvd., Barataria.* ☎ *800/741-1340. www.neworleansfishintours.com/lodging-info.html. 9 units (4–8 people per cabin/camp). All-inclusive fishing packages $350 per person (full-day chartered fishing tour, private accommodations, bait and tackle, all-you-can-eat breakfast, lunch, dinner, snacks, and drinks). AE, DISC, MC, V.*

Dining

kids Boutte's Bayou Restaurant. The scenic drive along the bayou, where you'll see shrimp boats and fishing camps, gives you an idea how important seafood is to this coastal community. My favorite dishes here are the shrimp po' boy, seafood gumbo, stuffed-shrimp plate, and fried catfish. Generous portions, friendly waitstaff, and local families make for a relaxed, satisfying meal. *5134 Boutte St., Lafitte.* ☎ *504/689-3889. Entrees $10–$15. AE, MC, V. Lunch Tues–Sun, dinner Thurs–Sun.*

★★★ Voleo's. Yes, everyone is staring at you as you enter this little dive on a dead-end street. Just take a seat at a checkered table, order Paul Prudhomme protégé David Volion's succulent flounder Lafitte, tap your toes to whatever's playing on the jukebox, and you'll stay out of trouble. *5134 Nunez St., Lafitte.* ☎ *504/689-2482. Entrees $10–$16. AE, DISC, MC, V. Mon, Wed–Sat 11am–9pm.*

A typical meal at Voleo's.

Plantations

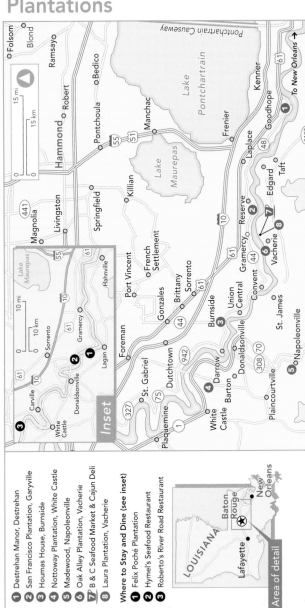

1 Destrehan Manor, Destrehan
2 San Francisco Plantation, Garyville
3 Houmas House, Burnside
4 Nottoway Plantation, White Castle
5 Madewood, Napoleonville
6 Oak Alley Plantation, Vacherie
7 B & C Seafood Market & Cajun Deli
8 Laura Plantation, Vacherie

Where to Stay and Dine (see inset)

1 Felix Poché Plantation
2 Hymel's Seafood Restaurant
3 Roberto's River Road Restaurant

Once plentiful and grand, southern Louisiana's plantation homes are now few and far between. During the most prosperous era of plantation life, from the 1820s to the beginning of the Civil War, white landowning families relied on slave labor to attain astonishing wealth. The homes are beautiful and uniquely atmospheric, though the specter of their shameful past will be omnipresent to some visitors. START: **From New Orleans, follow Interstate 10 west. Keep in mind that the river winds a bit, so some distances may be deceiving.**

1 Destrehan Plantation. If you saw *Interview with the Vampire*, you might recognize this elegant mansion built in 1787 by a free person of color as narrator Louis's (Brad Pitt's) childhood home. A meticulous restoration has given it new life, but one area was purposely left untouched so that you might better appreciate its survival. ⏱ *45 min. 13034 River Rd., Destrehan.* ☎ *877/453-2095 or 985/764-9315. www.destrehanplantation.org. Admission $18 adults, $7 children 6–16, free children 5 and under. Daily 9am–4pm.*

2 San Francisco Plantation. As you drive past a neighboring oil refinery, it's hard to imagine that this country home was once surrounded by sugar-cane fields. The whimsical architecture mimics a steamboat, but the bright yellow, blue, and pink hues are true to Creole heritage. Inside, look closely at the faux marble and faux wood, popular decorating effects at the time of its construction that demonstrated wealth. ⏱ *45 min. 2646 Hwy. 44, Garyville.* ☎ *888/322-1756 or 985/535-2341. www.sanfrancisco plantation.org. Admission $15 adults, $10 students, free children 6 and under. Daily 9:30am–5pm April–Oct; 9am–4pm Nov–March.*

3 Houmas House Plantation & Garden. Curiously, two homes—one dating back to 1790 and the other to 1840—were joined together under one roof to make up this enormous estate showcased on 38 acres (15 hectares) of huge live oaks, fragrant magnolias, and perfectly manicured formal gardens. The Bette Davis classic *Hush . . . Hush, Sweet Charlotte* was filmed here. ⏱ *1 hr. 40136 Hwy. 942, Burnside.* ☎ *888/323-8314 or 225/473-9380. www.houmashouse. com. Admission $20 adults, $15*

Some visitors may recognize Destrehan Plantation from the film Interview with the Vampire, *based on the Anne Rice novel.*

Houmas House.

children 13–18, $10 children 6-12, free children 5 and under; $10 garden tour only. Mon–Tues 9am–5pm, Wed–Sun 9am–8pm.

❹ ★★★ Nottoway Plantation and Resort. Known as the White Castle, Nottoway survived the Civil War because a Union officer had once stayed there as a guest; you can still see scars from shelling on some of the 22 columns. It's easy to get lost wandering among the mansion's 64 rooms sprawled across 54,000 square feet (5,016 sq. m). My favorite place is the pristine White Ballroom, with its original crystal chandeliers and spooky portrait of a grande dame whose eyes seem to follow you no matter where you go. ⊙ 90 min. 30970 Mississippi River Rd., White Castle. ☎ 866/LASOUTH (527-6884) or 225/545-2730. www.nottoway.com. Admission $20 adults, $6 children 6–12, free children 5 and under. Daily 9am–4pm.

❺ ★ Madewood Plantation. This place serves as a reminder that pettiness is never wise. It was originally built by a man who wanted to outshine his brother, but he died of yellow fever before it was finished. Current owners Keith Marshall and Millie Ball will gladly show you restoration photo albums detailing its transformation from 1960s wrecking-ball candidate to glorious Greek Revival masterpiece. ⊙ 1 hr. 4250 Hwy. 308, Napoleonville. ☎ 985/369-7151. www.madewood. com. Tours available for groups of 10 or more. Call for appointment and rates.

❻ ★ Oak Alley Plantation. The famous oak-lined drive nearly steals the thunder of this quintessential plantation home. Costumed docents complete the picture-perfect image, though their robotic recitations about its history make you wish you were free to explore on your own. There are also cottages for overnight stays. ⊙ 1 hr.

Oak Alley is the quintessential Southern plantation home.

3645 Hwy. 18, Vacherie. ☎ 800/44-ALLEY (442-5539) or 225/265-2151. www.oakalleyplantation.com. Admission $20 adults, $7.50 students, $4.50 children 6–12, free children 5 and under. Daily 9am–5pm Mar–Oct; Mon–Fri 9am–4:30pm, Sat–Sun 9am–5pm.

⑦ B & C Seafood Market & Cajun Deli. This family-owned and -operated joint is near Laura and Oak Alley. Order the seafood platter, filled with shrimp, oysters, catfish, and crawfish; save room for the bread pudding with sticky sweet rum sauce. 2155 Hwy. 18, Vacherie. ☎ 225/265-8356. $.

⑧ ★★★ Laura: A Creole Plantation. If you're only going to see one plantation, come here and be blown away by the docents' extensive knowledge and love for

Laura Plantation outbuildings.

this colorful 200-year-old Creole home and grounds. Unlike most plantation tours, they will share the slaves' stories as well and show you the slaves' and overseer's cabins, which were deliberately burned elsewhere so as to "forget" the past. ⓘ 90 min. 2247 Hwy. 18, Vacherie. ☎ 888/799-7690 or 225/265-7690. www.lauraplantation.com. Admission $20 adults, $6 children 6–17, free children 5 and under. Daily 10am–4pm.

Where to Stay & Dine

River Road is famous for its plantations and seafood. Squeezing in as many tours as you can in 1 day can be exhausting. Extend your visit to a night or two so you can enjoy the sights and food at your leisure.

Lodging

kids Felix Poché Plantation. This 1870 country Victorian home offers a shady porch with river breezes, a French Quarter–style pool, and 22 acres (8.8 hectares) to explore. The private cottages are nice but plain; stay in the main house instead if you prefer richer surroundings. Children are welcome. 6554 Hwy. 44 (River Rd.), Convent. ☎ 225/562-7728. www.pocheplantation.com. 8 units. Doubles $69–$249. AE, DISC, MC, V.

Poché Plantation dining room.

The Nottoway Plantation house.

★★★ Nottoway Plantation.

Stay the night if you dare; ghosts are rumored to roam the mansion. The most frequent sighting is that of a young auburn-haired woman in the girls' wing who resembles original owner John Randolph's youngest daughter, Julia Marceline. If you can afford it, sleep in the master bedroom, which boasts the Randolphs' original furniture, including a hand-carved rosewood poster bed with mosquito netting. Supposedly valuables were hidden in its hollow posts during the Civil War. A newly constructed replica carriage house and cottages are also available with modern amenities. *30970 Mississippi River Rd., White Castle.* ☎ *866/LASOUTH (527-6884) or 225/545-2730.* www. nottoway.com. *13 units. Doubles $190–$360. AE, MC, V.*

kids Oak Alley Plantation. View

the famous oak trees and National Historic Landmark home from your own private 19th-century cottage. Children are welcome. *3645 Hwy.18, Vacherie.* ☎ *800/44-ALLEY (442-5539) or 225/265-2151.* www. oakalleyplantation.com. *5 units. Doubles $130–$175 w/full country breakfast. AE, MC, V.*

Dining

★★ kids Hymel's Seafood

Restaurant. Owned and operated by the same family for more than 70 years, Hymel's is renowned for its fresh seafood. The warm, casual atmosphere and reasonable prices make it family-friendly, though it can get noisy at times. Be sure to order the SeaSpud potato, which is topped with real lump crab meat, boiled shrimp, and cheese. *8740 Hwy. 44, Convent.* ☎ *225/562-9910.* www.hymels.com. *Entrees $10–$30. MC, V. Tues–Fri 11am–2:30pm, Thurs 5–9pm, Fri 5–10pm, Sat 11am–10pm, Sun 11am–8pm.*

Roberto's River Road Restau-

rant. The restaurant might not look like much from the outside, but you'll immediately be wowed by the garlic spiciness of the River Road shrimp inside. *Located on the River Rd. (Hwy. 75) about 3 miles (4.8km) south of Gardere Lane and ¼ mile (.4km) north of Bayou Paul Lane, St. Gabriel.* ☎ *225/642-5999.* www.robertosrestaurant.net. *Entrees $15–$30. MC, V. Open Tues–Fri 11am–2pm, Tues–Thurs 5–9pm, Fri–Sat 5–10pm.* ●

Before You Go

Tourist Offices

New Orleans French Quarter: Visitor Information Center, 529 St. Ann St., New Orleans, LA 70116. ☎ 504/568-5661. Vieux Carré Police Station, 334 Royal St. ☎ 504/658-6080.

New Orleans Uptown: New Orleans Metropolitan Convention and Visitors Bureau, 2020 St. Charles Ave., New Orleans, LA 70130. ☎ 800/672-6124 or 504/566-5011; www.neworleanscvb.com.

New Orleans Downtown: New Orleans Multicultural Tourism Network, 2020 St. Charles Ave., New Orleans, LA 70130. ☎ 504/523-5652; www.soulofneworleans.com. Canal Street and Convention Center Boulevard ☎ 504/587-0739, at the beginning of the 300 block of Canal Street on the downtown side of the street. Walk-up booths at Julia Street and Convention Center Boulevard and Poydras Street and Convention Center Boulevard.

The Best Times to Go

Traditional seasons don't exist in southern Louisiana. (Local seafood lovers—myself included—insist that the only seasons that count are crawfish, shrimp, crab, and oyster.) In lieu of your plain ol' boring spring, summer, fall, and winter, New Orleans offers two extremes: a hot, humid summer (Apr–Nov) and a relatively mild winter (Dec–Mar).

If possible, avoid visiting the city in July and August, when temperatures soar into the 90s, thunderstorms pour down every afternoon, and the heat index makes the air feel like you're carrying an extra 20 pounds. Unless you plan on hunkering down in your air-conditioned

hotel room or watching countless movies in the cool comfort of a theater, the off-season summer deals aren't worth it. However, winter temps rarely dip below freezing. It's usually in the upper 60s in November, which makes for good walking weather, plus there's green grass and bright flowers year-round.

Hurricane season runs June 1 through November 30 so plan accordingly. August through October is when you see most tropical storm and hurricane action, so if that is a risk you'd rather not take, avoid those few months.

Festivals and Special Events

JAN. **Allstate Sugar Bowl Classic** (☎ 504/828-2440; www.allstate sugarbowl.org) attracts die-hard college football fans from all over the country.

FEB. On **Mardi Gras day** (☎ 800/672-6124 or 504/566-5011; www.mardigrasday.com), the entire city is just one big party. The date varies from year to year, but it always falls 46 days before Easter.

MAR. **The Tennessee Williams New Orleans Literary Festival** (☎ 504/581-1144; www.tennessee williams.net) features readings, theater performances, workshops, and more in honor of Williams, an honorary New Orleanian.

APR. The **French Quarter Festival** (☎ 504/522-5730; www.fqfi.org) is a huge free music and food fest that warms up crowds for the more famous **Jazz Fest,** aka the **New Orleans Jazz & Heritage Festival** (☎ 504/410-4100; www.nojazzfest. com). For Jazz Fest, the Fair Grounds Race Course is transformed into a mass of music stages

Previous page: The St. Charles streetcar.

featuring everything from blues to pop to R & B by little local bands and best-selling artists.

JUL. Essence Music Festival (☎ 504/523-5652; www.essence.com/festival) celebrates African-American culture with music and self-improvement workshops.

SEP. Southern Decadence (☎ 504/522-8047; www.southerndecadence.net) brings the gay community together for parades, costume contests, and more.

NOV–DEC. The **Celebration in the Oaks** (☎ 504/483-9415; www.celebrationintheoaks.com) is a festival of lights set among the giant oaks that can be viewed on foot, by car, or by miniature-train ride.

Cell Phones

In general it's a good bet that your phone will work in New Orleans, on either **CDMA** or **GSM** wireless networks; in fact, the largest wireless providers (that is, Verizon, AT&T, and T-Mobile) in the region have upgraded their data networks to the new higher-speed "4G" (fourth-generation wireless) standard (available only on compatible phones). However, foreign visitors may or may not be able to send SMS (text messages) overseas or receive and send data at 4G speeds. Assume nothing—call your wireless provider and get the full scoop.

You can always rent a phone from **InTouch USA** (☎ 800/872-7626; www.intouchglobal.com), but beware that you'll pay $1 a minute or more for airtime.

Car Rental

If you plan to hang out in the French Quarter, you're better off walking or taking a cab. It's hard to find parking plus it's expensive. If you truly need a rental car, the best deals are usually found at rental-car company websites, although all the major online travel agencies also offer rental-car reservations services. Priceline and Hotwire work well for rental cars too; the only mystery is which major rental company you get, although for most travelers the difference between Hertz, Avis, and Budget is negligible.

Getting **There**

By Plane

If you fly into New Orleans, you arrive at Louis Armstrong International Airport (Internet airport code MSY), about 25 minutes outside the city. It's smaller than most bus stations, so you'll find it an easy walk to baggage claim and a taxi stand.

Getting into Town from the Airport

By Cab

A taxi ride to the French Quarter from the airport will cost you $33 for one or two people and an additional $14 each for three or more people.

United Cab (☎ 504/524-9606; www.unitedcabs.com) is my favorite cab company because they're professional and friendly. I also recommend Metry Cab (☎ 504/835-4242 www.metrycab.com). Both companies take credit cards. Please remember to tip 10% to 15% for good service.

By Shuttle Bus

A cab might be more convenient, but if you prefer a cheaper shuttle bus, go to one of the 24-hour info desks in the airport for a schedule.

For $2, the Downtown/Airport Express bus takes you to the corner of Carrollton and Tulane avenues—a 30- to 40-minute ride. The bus leaves from the upper level near the down ramp about every 20 minutes from 5:30am to midnight (every 12–15 min. during rush hours). The Jefferson Transit Authority (☎ 504/818-1077; www.jeffersontransit.org) can give you more information.

For $20 (one-way), the Airport Shuttle takes you directly to your hotel from right outside the baggage area. For a reservation, call ☎ 504/522-3500. The shuttle is wheelchair accessible.

By Car
If you drive to New Orleans, you'll take one of the major thoroughfares: the Pontchartrain Expressway (Hwy.) 90 or Interstate 10. The former is best if you're heading to the Garden District or Warehouse District; the latter if your destination is Uptown or the French Quarter.

By Train
Your train will arrive at the Union Passenger Terminal, 1001 Loyola Ave. (☎ 800/USA-RAIL or 504/528-1610; www.amtrak.com) in the Central Business District, just a few blocks from the French Quarter. (Interesting side note: the station temporarily served as a post-Katrina jail). Taxis are readily available outside.

Getting Around

On Foot
The city is flat, which makes it perfect for walking. Just keep an eye out for large oak-tree roots, which make for roller-coaster sidewalks.

By Public Transportation
Call the Regional Transit Authority's Ride Line at ☎ 504/248-3900 for maps, passes, and other information about streetcars or buses. Any of New Orleans's visitor information centers (including the main location at 529 St. Ann St. by Jackson Square) also have information on public transportation.

The Jazzy Pass is a fantastic deal if you frequently use public transportation. It's available at Walgreens drugstores, hotels, and banks in the Quarter, Central Business District, and along Canal Street in 1-day ($5), 3-day ($12), or 5-day ($20) increments. For more information contact the New Orleans Regional Transit Authority

(NORTA; ☎ 504/248-3900; www.norta.com).

By Streetcar
Since 1835, the St. Charles streetcar line has serviced the Central Business District, Garden District, Lower Garden District, Uptown, and Carrollton neighborhoods. The Canal streetcar line is a 5½-mile (8.9km) ride up Canal through the Central Business District and Mid-City, and ends at one of two destinations, either north on the Carrollton spur to the 1,500-acre (600-hectare) City Park or farther west to the Cypress Grove and Greenwood cemeteries. Both streetcars operate 24 hours a day. Riding either streetcar costs just $1.25 each way (exact change or a Jazzy Pass is required). The Riverfront streetcar line runs along the riverfront from the Convention Center to the French Quarter at Esplanade Avenue. It costs $1.50 (exact change or a Jazzy Pass is

required). Only the Canal and Riverfront streetcars are wheelchair accessible.

By Bus

Buses connect most New Orleans neighborhoods, though depending on your destination, you'd do best to take the more scenic streetcar when possible. Bus fare is $1.25 (exact change or a Jazzy Pass is required). Transfers cost 25¢, and buses are wheelchair accessible.

By Taxi

After dark, I strongly suggest you go with a cab instead of public transportation. Unless it's rush hour, they're easy to find in the French Quarter, though you might want to call ahead if you're in a rush. Rates are $3.50 initial charge, plus $2 per mile (25¢ per 1/8 mile) thereafter. Add $1 for each additional person. The maximum number of

passengers is five. Many cabs take credit cards, but ask before your driver starts the meter.

By Bike

Because the city is flat, you don't need to be Lance Armstrong to bike around. Bicycle Michael's (☎ 504/945-9505; www.bicycle michaels.com) and American Bicycle Rentals (☎ 866/293-4037) are two good bets for rentals. For maps of bike trails, visit the New Orleans Bicycle Club at www.neworleans bicycleclub.org.

By Car

To drive in New Orleans is to be masochistic. Parking is a pain, finding your way is tough because the city's streets follow the twists and turns of the river, and local drivers often make last-minute lane changes and exits. Avoid it if at all possible.

Fast Facts

AREA CODE The area code for the greater New Orleans metropolitan area is 504. The North Shore, the region north of the city across Lake Pontchartrain, which includes Slidell, Covington, and Mandeville, is 985.

ATMS/CASH POINTS The **Cirrus** (☎ 800/424-7787; www.mastercard. com) and **PLUS** (☎ 800/843-7587; www.visa.com) networks span the globe; look at the back of your bank card to see which network you're on, then call or check online for automated teller machine (ATM) locations in New Orleans (they're found all over the city so you shouldn't have trouble finding one).

Be sure to find out your daily withdrawal limit before you depart. Also keep in mind that many banks impose a fee every time a card is

used at a different bank's ATM, and that fee can be higher for international transactions (up to $5 or more) than for domestic ones (where they're rarely more than $1.50).

Note: Some small establishments in New Orleans won't take credit cards, so it's always wise to carry a small amount of cash on you.

BABYSITTERS Ask your hotel or call one of the following agencies for sitting services: **Accents on Children's Arrangements** (☎ 800/539-1227; www.accentoca.com), or **Dependable Kid Care** (☎ 504/486-5044; www.dependable care.net).

BUSINESS HOURS On the whole, most shops and stores are open from 10am to 6pm. Banks open at 9am and close between 3 and 5pm.

CAMERA REPAIR Try **AAA Camera Repair,** 1631 St. Charles Ave. (☎ 504/561-5822).

CONVENTION CENTER **Ernest M. Morial Convention Center,** 900 Convention Center Blvd., New Orleans, LA 70130, ☎ 504/582-3000; www.mccno.com. Convention Center Boulevard sits at the end of the Warehouse District, on the river between Thalia and Water streets; the Riverfront streetcar drops you off at the Convention Center.

DENTISTS Contact the **New Orleans Dental Association** (☎ 504/834-6449; www.nodental. org) to find a recommended dentist near you.

DOCTORS If you need a doctor, call one of the following: **Ochsner Baptist Medical Center,** ☎ 504/899-9311, or **Tulane University Medical Center,** ☎ 504/588-5800.

EMBASSIES & CONSULATES All embassies are located in the nation's capital, Washington, D.C. If your country isn't listed below, call for directory information in Washington, D.C. (☎ 202/555-1212), or log on to www.embassy.org/embassies. The embassy of **Australia** is at 1601 Massachusetts Ave. NW, Washington, DC 20036 (☎ 202/797-3000; www.australia. visahq.com). The embassy of **Canada** is at 501 Pennsylvania Ave. NW, Washington, DC 20001 (☎ 202/682-1740; www.canadian embassy.org). The embassy of **Ireland** is at 2234 Massachusetts Ave. NW, Washington, DC 20008 (☎ 202/462-3939; www.embassy ofireland.org). The embassy of **New Zealand** is at 37 Observatory Circle NW, Washington, DC 20008 (☎ 202/328-4800; www.nzembassy. com). The embassy of the **United Kingdom** is at 3100 Massachusetts

Ave. NW, Washington, DC 20008 (☎ 202/588-6500; http://ukinusa. fco.gov.uk).

EMERGENCIES For fire, police, and ambulance call ☎ 911. For the **Poison Control Center,** call ☎ 800/222-1222. The **Travelers Aid Society** (1615 Canal St., Suite B; ☎ 504/586-0010) renders emergency aid to travelers in need. For help regarding a missing or lost child, call **Child Find of America** at ☎ 800/IAM-LOST (426-5678). If a hurricane threatens, ask your hotel concierge to help you arrange for transportation out of the city. Most hotels no longer allow guests or even their employees to ride out the storm.

GAY & LESBIAN TRAVELERS Gays and lesbians are a vibrant part of New Orleans culture. For information on what's going on in the LGBT community in New Orleans, check out www.gayneworleans. com, and Ambush Magazine (☎ 504/522-8049; www.ambush mag.com).

HOLIDAYS Banks, government offices, and post offices are closed on the following legal national holidays: January 1 (New Year's Day), the third Monday in January (Martin Luther King, Jr. Day), the third Monday in February (Presidents Day), the last Monday in May (Memorial Day), July 4 (Independence Day), the first Monday in September (Labor Day), the second Monday in October (Columbus Day), November 11 (Veterans Day), the fourth Thursday in November (Thanksgiving Day), and December 25 (Christmas). Also, the Tuesday following the first Monday in November is Election Day and is a federal government holiday in presidential-election years (held every 4 years, and next in 2016). Stores, museums, and restaurants are open most holidays, except for

Thanksgiving, Christmas, and New Year's Day.

Note: Mardi Gras day is considered a holiday in the greater New Orleans area, and most businesses are closed or have shortened hours.

HOSPITALS Should you become ill during your visit, most major hospitals have staff doctors on call 24 hours a day. However, there are fewer physicians post-Katrina, so after-hours health care may be more limited or require longer waiting periods. If a doctor isn't available in your hotel or guesthouse, call or go to the emergency room at Ochsner Medical Center, 1516 Jefferson Hwy. (☎ 504/842-3000).

HOT LINES **Louisiana Rape Crisis** is ☎ 800/656-4673; **Travelers Aid Society** is ☎ 504/586-0010; **Gamblers Anonymous** is ☎ 504/431-7867; **Narcotics Anonymous** is ☎ 504/899-6262; **Alcoholics Anonymous** is ☎ 504/838-3399.

INFORMATION The local **Tourist Information Center** is at 529 St. Ann St. (☎ 504/568-5661 or 504/566-5031).

INSURANCE **Trip-Cancellation Insurance:** Trip-cancellation insurance helps you get your money back if you have to back out of a trip, if you have to go home early, or if your travel supplier goes bankrupt. Allowed reasons for cancellation can range from sickness to natural disasters to the State Department declaring your destination unsafe for travel. (Insurers usually won't cover vague fears, though.) In this unstable world, trip-cancellation insurance is a good buy if you're getting tickets well in advance. Insurance policy details vary, so read the fine print—and especially make sure that your airline is on the list of carriers covered in case of bankruptcy. For information, contact one of the following insurers: **Access America**

(☎ 866/807-3982; www.access america.com), **Travel Guard International** (☎ 800/826-4919; www.travelguard.com), **Travel Insured International** (☎ 800/243-3174; www.travelinsured.com), or **Travelex Insurance Services** (☎ 888/457-4602; www.travel exinsurance.com).

Medical Insurance: Although it's not required of travelers, health insurance is highly recommended. Unlike many European countries, the United States does not usually offer free or low-cost medical care to its citizens or visitors. Doctors and hospitals are expensive, and in most cases will require advance payment or proof of coverage before they render their services. Though lack of health insurance may prevent you from being admitted to a hospital in nonemergencies, don't worry about being left on a street corner to die: The American way is to fix you now and bill the living daylights out of you later.

For British Travelers: Most big travel agents offer their own insurance and will probably try to sell you their package when you book a holiday. Think before you sign. **The Association of British Insurers** (☎ 020/7600-3333; www.abi.org.uk) gives advice by phone and publishes *Holiday Insurance,* a free guide to policy provisions and prices. You might also shop around for better deals: Try **Columbus Direct** (☎ 020/7375-0011; www.columbusdirect.net).

For Canadian Travelers: Canadians should check with their provincial health plan offices or call **Health Canada** (☎ 613/957-2991; www.hc-sc.gc.ca) to find out the extent of coverage and what documentation and receipts must be taken home if they are treated in the United States.

Lost-Luggage Insurance: On domestic flights, checked baggage is covered up to $3,000 per ticketed passenger. On international flights (including U.S. portions of international trips), baggage is limited to approximately $9 per pound (1.1kg), up to approximately $635 per checked bag. If you plan to check items more valuable than the standard liability, see if your valuables are covered by your homeowner's policy, or get baggage insurance as part of your comprehensive travel-insurance package. Don't buy insurance at the airport, as it's usually overpriced. Be sure to take any valuables or irreplaceable items with you in your carry-on luggage, since many valuables (including books, money, and electronics) aren't covered by airline policies.

If your luggage is lost, immediately file a lost-luggage claim at the airport, detailing the luggage contents. For most airlines, you must report delayed, damaged, or lost baggage within 4 hours of arrival. The airlines are required to deliver luggage, once found, directly to your house or destination free of charge.

INTERNET ACCESS Most hotels and cafes and all Starbucks offer free Wi-Fi. Go to www.jiwire.com for more public Wi-Fi options.

LIQUOR LAWS The legal drinking age in New Orleans is 21. You can buy liquor most anywhere 24 hours a day, 7 days a week, 365 days a year. All drinks carried on the street must be in plastic cups; bars often provide one of these plastic "go-cups" so that you can transfer your drink as you leave.

LOST & FOUND Be sure to notify all your credit card companies the minute you discover your wallet has been lost or stolen, and file a report at the nearest police precinct (☎ 311). Your insurance company may require a police report before covering any claims. Most credit card companies have an emergency toll-free number to call if your card is lost or stolen; they may be able to wire you a cash advance immediately or deliver an emergency credit card in a day or two. **Visa's** U.S. emergency number is ☎ 800/847-2911 or 410/581-9994. **American Express** cardholders should call ☎ 800/221-7282. **MasterCard** holders should call ☎ 800/307-7309 or 636/722-7111. For other credit cards, call the toll-free number directory at ☎ 800/555-1212. If you need emergency cash over the weekend, when all banks and American Express offices are closed, you can have money wired to you via **Western Union** (☎ 800/325-6000; www.westernunion.com).

If you lost something at the airport, call **Airport Operations** (☎ 504/464-2671 or -2672). If you lost something at a security checkpoint, call the **Support Operations Center** at ☎ 504/463-2252. If you lost something on the **bus,** call ☎ 504/940-5586, or on the **streetcar,** call ☎ 504/827-8399. If you lost something anywhere else, phone the **New Orleans Police Non-Emergency line** (☎ 504/821-2222). You may also want to fill out a police report for insurance purposes.

MAIL The main post office is at 701 Loyola Ave. In the French Quarter, there is one at 1022 Iberville.

NEWSPAPERS & MAGAZINES To find out what's going on around town, pick up a copy of the *Times-Picayune* (www.nola.com) or *Gambit* (www.bestofneworleans.com). *OffBeat* (www.offbeat.com) is a comprehensive monthly guide to the city's evening entertainment, art galleries, and special events; it's available in most hotels.

Useful Websites

- **Times-Picayune** (local newspaper): www.nola.com
- **The Gambit** (local alt-weekly): www.bestofneworleans.com
- **Offbeat** (monthly entertainment guide): www.offbeat.com
- **Travel guides for families:** www.neworleansonline.com/neworleans/family
- **Out Traveler** (gay & lesbian travel guide): www.outtraveler.com
- **Weather reports:** www.accuweather.com, www.weather.com

PARKING In the French Quarter, you're better off in a pricey parking lot rather than risk an illegal spot. If you park on a parade route or block someone's driveway, your car will be towed to the impounding lot (☎ 504/565-7235) or the Claiborne Auto Pound, 400 N. Claiborne Ave. (☎ 504/565-7450). Prepare to pay a hefty fine of $100 or more.

PASSPORTS **For Residents of Australia:** You can pick up an application from your local post office or any branch of Passports Australia, but you must schedule an interview at the passport office to present your application materials. Call the **Australian Passport Information Service** at ☎ 131-232, or visit the government website at www.passports.gov.au.

For Residents of Canada: Passport applications are available at travel agencies throughout Canada or from the central **Passport Office,** Department of Foreign Affairs and International Trade, Ottawa, ON K1A 0G3 (☎ 800/567-6868; www.ppt.gc.ca).

For Residents of Ireland: You can apply for a 10-year passport at the **Passport Office,** Setanta Centre, Molesworth Street, Dublin 2 (☎ 01/671-1633; www.irlgov.ie/iveagh). Those under age 18 and over 65 must apply for a 3-year passport. You can also apply at 1A South Mall, Cork (☎ 021/272-525), or at most main post offices.

For Residents of New Zealand: You can pick up a passport application at any New Zealand Passports Office or download it from their website. Contact the **Passports Office** at ☎ 0800/225-050 in New Zealand or 04/474-8100, or log on to www.passports.govt.nz.

For Residents of the United Kingdom: To pick up an application for a standard 10-year passport (5-year passport for children under 16), visit your nearest passport office, major post office, or travel agency, or contact the **United Kingdom Passport Service** at ☎ 0870/521-0410, or search its website at www.ukpa.gov.uk.

International visitors to New Orleans should always keep a photocopy of their passport with them. If your passport is lost or stolen, having a copy significantly facilitates the reissuing process at a local consulate or embassy. Keep your passport and other valuables in your room's safe or in the hotel safe.

PHARMACIES The **Walgreens Drug Store** at 1801 St. Charles Ave. (☎ 504/561-8458) is the closest one to the French Quarter that offers 24-hour pharmacy service.

POLICE For nonemergency situations, call ☎ 504/821-2222. For emergencies, dial ☎ 911.

RADIO STATIONS Popular radio stations include WSMB, 1350 AM (sports talk); WWNO, 89.9 FM (National Public Radio, classical); WWOZ, 90.7 FM (New Orleans and Louisiana music; jazz, R & B, and blues); WQUE, 93.3 FM (urban/R & B); and KMEZ, 106.7 FM (old-school/contemporary R & B). For local news, tune in to talk radio station WWL, 870 AM.

RESTROOMS Public restrooms are located at Jax Brewery, the Outlet Collection at Riverwalk, the Shops at Canal Place, Washington Artillery Park, and major hotels.

SAFETY New Orleans's neighborhoods can change from block to block so always be aware of your surroundings. Women should consider substituting a backpack for your usual purse or simply don't carry one. Public transportation is fine during the day but a cab is best at night. Avoid St. Louis Cemetery No. 2 near Claiborne on the lake side of the Iberville Housing Project unless you're traveling with a large tour group. Also stay away from the area behind Armstrong Park.

TAXES In general, the total sales tax in New Orleans is 9% (13% for hotel stays); it's 8.75% in Jefferson Parish.

TELEPHONES For directory assistance ("information"), dial ☎ 411. Hotel surcharges on long-distance and local calls are astronomical, so you're usually better off using a cell or public pay telephone.

TIME ZONE New Orleans is in the Central Standard Time (CST) zone. Daylight saving time is in effect from the second Sunday in March through the first Sunday in November.

TIPPING In hotels, tip bellhops at least $1 per bag and tip the chamber staff $1 to $2 per day (more if you've left a disaster area); the doorman or concierge only if he or she has provided you with some specific service. Tip the valet-parking attendant $1 every time you get your car. In restaurants, bars, and nightclubs, service staff and bartenders expect 15% to 20% of the check, checkroom attendants $1 per garment, and valet-parking attendants $1 per vehicle. Tip cab drivers 15%, skycaps at least $1 per bag, and hairdressers and barbers 15% to 20%.

TRAVELERS WITH DISABILITIES Organizations that offer a vast range of resources and assistance to travelers with disabilities include **MossRehab** (☎ 800/CALL-MOSS; www.mossresourcenet.org); the **American Foundation for the Blind** (AFB; ☎ 800/232-5463; www. afb.org); and **SATH** (Society for Accessible Travel & Hospitality; ☎ 212/447-7284; www.sath.org). AirAmbulanceCard.com is now partnered with SATH and allows you to preselect top-notch hospitals in case of an emergency. **Access-Able Travel Source** (☎ 303/232-2979; www.access-able.com) offers a comprehensive database on travel agents from around the world with experience in accessible travel; destination-specific access information; and links to such resources as service animals, equipment rentals, and access guides.

Many travel agencies offer customized tours and itineraries for travelers with disabilities. Among them are Flying Wheels Travel (☎ 507/451-5005; www.flying wheelstravel.com) and Accessible Journeys (☎ 800/846-4537 or 610/521-0339; www.disabilitytravel. com).

British travelers should contact Holiday Care (📞 0845-124-9971 in U.K. only; www.tourismforall.org.uk)

to access a wide range of travel information and resources for seniors and travelers with disabilities.

New Orleans: **A Brief History**

1682 French explorer René-Robert Cavelier, Sieur de LaSalle, claims the land near the mouth of the Mississippi and dubs it Louisiana in honor of King Louis XIV.

1718 New Orleans is founded as a valuable port city by Pierre Le Moyne, Sieur d'Iberville, and named in honor of Philippe, Duc d'Orléans.

1762–1800 After Louis XIV gave Louisiana to his Spanish cousin, King Charles III, the French Quarter burned down twice, which explains the Spanish influence on architecture.

1794 Pioneering farmer Etienne de Boré invents a way to extract sugar from cane, which remains a boon crop to this day.

1800 Louisiana is returned to the French.

1803 Napoleon secretly sells the Louisiana territory to the United States, best known today as the Louisiana Purchase.

1805 The city of New Orleans officially incorporates.

1812 Louisiana becomes the 18th state of the United States of America.

1815 Battle of New Orleans is a pivotal moment in defeating the British for good in the War of 1812.

1832–33 More than 10,000 citizens die during the horrific yellow fever and cholera epidemics.

1837 Mardi Gras is reported on for the first time by the press.

1840 In its glory, New Orleans is the fourth largest city in the country and the second largest port city after New York.

1850 The rampant slave trade makes New Orleans the largest slave market in the nation.

1862 New Orleans is captured by Union soldiers.

1865–77 Time of Reconstruction, when carpetbaggers come in droves and change the city's social and economic dynamic.

1890 Arrested for boarding the "wrong" train, Homer Plessy decides to sue the state, paving the way for the landmark segregation legislation *Plessy v. Ferguson*.

1892 The St. Charles streetcar goes electric.

1900 Birth of Louis Armstrong, iconic musician, actor, and informal ambassador of all things New Orleans.

1928 Radical populist Huey P. "Kingfish" Long becomes governor of Louisiana, and is then elected to the U.S. Senate 4 years later.

1935 Long is shot at the Louisiana Capitol in Baton Rouge and dies 2 days later at the age of 42.

1938 Playwright Tennessee Williams moves to the Crescent City.

1956 Lake Pontchartrain Causeway, the world's longest bridge, is completed.

1960 Integration of public schools.

1964 The original Canal streetcar is replaced with buses, which are hit with tomatoes by protesting locals.

Learn the Lingo

Talking the talk and walking the walk are crucial if you plan to go to New Orleans during Mardi Gras. Here's how to sound like a native:

- **Ball** or **Tableau Ball:** Krewes host these themed, masked balls. Themes change from year to year.
- **Boeuf Gras** (fattened calf): The calf represents ritual sacrifice, as well as the last meal eaten before Lent, the Roman-Catholic season of fasting leading up to Easter. It's also the symbol of Mardi Gras and the first float of the Rex parade.
- **Carnival:** A celebration beginning January 6 (the 12th night after Christmas) and ending Mardi Gras day.
- **Court:** A krewe's king, queen, and attendants.
- **Doubloon:** Krewes throw these metal coins during parades. They feature the logo of the krewe on one side and its theme for a particular year on the other.
- **Fat Tuesday:** Otherwise known as Mardi Gras, the last day before Ash Wednesday, which is the first day of Lent.
- **Favor:** Krewe members give these souvenirs, which feature the krewe's logo and date, to people who attend their ball.
- **Flambeaux:** Flaming torches carried by parade marchers who aren't members of the krewe.
- **King Cake:** An oval, sugared pastry decorated with purple, green, and gold (Mardi Gras colors) that contains a small doll representing the infant Jesus.
- **Krewe:** The traditional word for a Carnival organization.
- **Lagniappe** (pronounced lan-yap): Loosely means "a little extra," and refers to any small gift or token, even a scrap of food or a free drink.
- **Mardi Gras:** French for "Fat Tuesday." Technically, if you say "Mardi Gras day," you're really saying "Fat Tuesday day."
- **Rex:** Latin for "king." The King of Carnival is Rex.
- **Second Line:** A group of people that follows a parade, dancing to the music. Also, a musical term that specifies a particular shuffling tempo popularized in much of New Orleans music.
- **Throws:** Inexpensive trinkets thrown from floats to parade watchers, including doubloons, minifootballs, plastic swords, spears, and all sorts of knickknacks. The most coveted throws are the gilded coconuts of the Zulu Social Aid and Pleasure Club.

1975 Louisiana Superdome opens with great fanfare and mixed reaction.

1977 Ernest N. "Dutch" Morial is elected as the city's first African-American mayor.

1984 Redevelopment inspired by the Louisiana World Expo helps the local economy during the dramatic '80s oil bust.

2000 The National World War II Museum opens.

2004 The Canal streetcar reopens with air-conditioned, handicapped-accessible red cars.

2005 Multiple levees break during Hurricane Katrina, destroying a large portion of New Orleans and killing 1,833 people throughout the southern U.S.

2010 British Petroleum's oil rig *Deepwater* Horizon explodes and sinks, killing 11 workers and discharging 4.9 million barrels of oil into the Gulf of Mexico.

Index

See also Accommodations and Restaurant indexes, below.

Restaurants

Photo **Credits**

Notes

[10]